John's Gospel

Who Is Jesus?

A Devotional

TS Taylor

All for the Glory of God

Original Cover Artwork: Pixabay - betidraws

Scripture is taken from the New King James Version®.
Copyright © 1982 by Thomas Nelson. Used by
permission. All rights reserved.

Printed in the United States of America

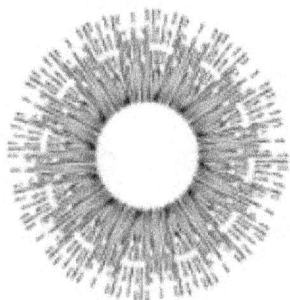

Other Books by TS Taylor:

Life-Changing Devotionals

The Love and Mercy of God as Seen in Jonah, Job, and Joseph

Flight to Freedom, Laws to Live By, How to Worship

Exodus Devotionals

High and Lifted Up – Is God Still Engaged in His World?

Isaiah Devotionals

Walk with Jesus and His Followers

Matthew Devotionals

Life Applications from Romans

Romans Devotionals

Scientific Faith

How to Bridge the Gap Between Faith and Science – Small Group Study Book

Reflections on Faith and Science from Genesis to Current Events

Reflect on some of the deeper issues of life

Luke's Gospel

Eyewitness Account Devotionals

Reflections on The Psalms, Book1

Learning to Love God More Deeply

Reflections on The Psalms, Book2

Learning to Love God More Deeply

Reflections on Forgiveness

What Does the Bible Tell Us About Forgiveness?

What About…?

Interesting Thoughts in the Bible

"For God so loved the world that He gave His only begotten Son, that whoever believes in Him should not perish but have everlasting life." (John 3:16)

Introduction

This is a different style of devotional. You will get to see Jesus in a different light, so go at your own pace through this devotional. I hope that you too will learn some new ways of thinking and living; that these encounters with Jesus will show you more about the Light of the World, the Way, the Truth, and the Life.

Tom S Taylor

In The Beginning - John 1:1-5

John begins his gospel very differently than Matthew, Mark, and Luke begin theirs. They all talk about Jesus' life beginning on the Earth. John has a very different perspective.

> *1 In the beginning was the Word, and the Word was with God, and the Word was God. 2 He was in the beginning with God. 3 All things were made through Him, and without Him nothing was made that was made. 4 In Him was life, and the life was the light of men. 5 And the light shines in the darkness, and the darkness did not comprehend it. (John 1:1-5)*

John begins at the very beginning, before the creation of all that is. John refers to Jesus as the *logos*, the Word. *Logos* is the Greek word from which we get our words for logic and reason. This *logos* is not some impersonal force, but He is described as a person who creates. He makes life and light. John reflects back to the opening words in the Book of Genesis.

> *1 In the beginning God created the heavens and the earth. 2 The earth was without form, and void; and darkness was on the face of the deep. And the Spirit of God was hovering over the face of the waters.*
>
> *3 Then God said, "Let there be light"; and there was light. 4 And God saw the light,*

that it was good; and God divided the light from the darkness. ⁵ God called the light Day, and the darkness He called Night. So the evening and the morning were the first day. (Genesis 1:1-5)

Both sections of Scripture talk about creating. They both speak of light and darkness. John writes to clearly show who this *Logos* is. He is God. He is involved in the beginning of creation. He is the giver of life and light. He will bring light and meaning to the world, beyond what normal darkness can comprehend. The Creation was created by God speaking, by the Word of God.

John's introduction shows that he is going to go into depth on who Jesus is and what His purpose is, for he states near the end of his Gospel:

...but these are written that you may believe that Jesus is the Christ, the Son of God, and that believing you may have life in His name. (John 20:31)

If you are interested in understanding what real life is about, come and join us, for He is the light of life; for all of us.

Notes:

Children of God - John 1:6-13

John, the writer, quickly switches to John the Baptist, to tell his part in the story of Jesus. John is making it clear that his role is just to point to the Light.

6 There was a man sent from God, whose name was John. 7 This man came for a witness, to bear witness of the Light, that all through him might believe. 8 He was not that Light, but was sent to bear witness of that Light. 9 That was the true Light which gives light to every man coming into the world.

10 He was in the world, and the world was made through Him, and the world did not know Him. 11 He came to His own, and His own did not receive Him. 12 But as many as received Him, to them He gave the right to become children of God, to those who believe in His name: 13 who were born, not of blood, nor of the will of the flesh, nor of the will of man, but of God. (John 1:6-13)

John is sent from God as a messenger, a prophet. His task is to point out the Light. Everyone wants to know about the Light. John tells them that He made all that is and now He is coming here, to the Earth to be with His people. Unfortunately, many do not receive Him as Light and Life. However, if you do receive Him, He will make sure that you are adopted into God's family. You will become a son or daughter of God.

You do not have to "do anything" to be adopted into God's family. You only need to believe in His name. You need to confess that your way is not making it in life. When you feel that you are stumbling in the dark, you need to reach out to the Light. It will be like you are born into a new family.

This was very radical language in Jesus' time. The idea of God adopting us into His family, as His children, is not based on how good we try to be, or how hard we work at it, but by belief. As we will see many people in Jesus' time had trouble believing this.

The same is true today. God wants to adopt us into His family, to be His children. We can be born of God through His will and the work of His Son, Jesus.

Do you know someone who needs to be adopted into a bigger, better family? Someone who is incredibly lonely. Someone who is lost in the dark? If so, ask them if they would like to read through the Gospel of John with you. What is stopping you? John promises that it will be quite a journey!

Notes:

He Has Seen God - John 1:14-18

John continues to expand on who the logos, the Word, is. The Word who was with God the Father from the beginning, at the time of creation, comes into the world.

14 And the Word became flesh and dwelt among us, and we beheld His glory, the glory as of the only begotten of the Father, full of grace and truth.

15 John bore witness of Him and cried out, saying, "This was He of whom I said, 'He who comes after me is preferred before me, for He was before me.' "

16 And of His fullness we have all received, and grace for grace. 17 For the law was given through Moses, but grace and truth came through Jesus Christ. 18 No one has seen God at any time. The only begotten Son, who is in the bosom of the Father, He has declared Him. (John 1:14-18)

In John's version of Jesus coming into the world, there is no baby in the manger, no angels singing to the shepherds, and no wise men come and visit the baby Jesus. John tells us that Jesus became flesh and dwelt among us. He became one of us. He experienced hunger, thirst, and exhaustion.

John describes Him as the One who was before John. He brings grace. He is here to fulfill the Law. He is here to show us the truth of God's Law. Moses was just the messenger of the Law, but Jesus is here to bring grace and truth.

Jesus is here to tell us about God the Father because He knows God the Father. Jesus came from God's throne room, the place of power, and He also comes from God's bosom, the place of lovingkindness.

Intellectuals often sit around and discuss what God must be like. But, how can they know? The best they can bring to the discussion is learning about God from His creation. Jesus says that if you want to know what God is like, come to Him. He knows and He will not only show you the truth of who God is, but He will also show you about God's grace.

The scenes of the manager, angels, and wise men are important; but they just point to the One who was with God the Father before time existed, and now has come as flesh to dwell among us. This is so we can learn about who God is.

Jesus asks you to start with Himself, the One who is truly God and truly man. He can lead you back to God's bosom. What would it feel like if you were resting in the bosom of God the Father? Take a minute to imagine what that would be like.

Notes:

The Lamb of God - John 1:29-34

John the Baptist is baptizing in the Jordan River. He is the voice crying in the wilderness, pointing the way to the One who brings Light and Truth. The next day Jesus shows up.

29 The next day John saw Jesus coming toward him, and said, "Behold! The Lamb of God who takes away the sin of the world! 30 This is He of whom I said, 'After me comes a Man who is preferred before me, for He was before me.' 31 I did not know Him; but that He should be revealed to Israel, therefore I came baptizing with water."

32 And John bore witness, saying, "I saw the Spirit descending from heaven like a dove, and He remained upon Him. 33 I did not know Him, but He who sent me to baptize with water said to me, 'Upon whom you see the Spirit descending, and remaining on Him, this is He who baptizes with the Holy Spirit.' 34 And I have seen and testified that this is the Son of God." (John 1:29-34)

John declared to all of the religious leaders that Jesus was the Lamb of God. This was an incredibly powerful image for the Jewish leaders. For they all knew that once a year on the day of Atonement, the High Priest would lay his hands on the sacrificial lamb. Then, the lamb was then driven out into the wilderness to die for the sins of the people.

Jesus, as the Lamb of God, existed before John and yet He submits to become flesh to be among His people.

John testifies that he sees the Holy Spirit in the form of a dove descending from God the Father to remain on Jesus. Here we see an unveiling of the trinity; Father, Son, and Holy Spirit.

Jesus is getting ready to begin His earthly ministry. How do you think it will go? Will everyone listen to Jesus and accept Him? (No). Will everyone run to His light and leave the darkness? (No). Will everyone understand the truth that He brings? Will everyone take on His grace? (No and no.) Yet, Jesus begins His three-year ministry. He is here to be Light and Truth and He is here as the Lamb of God. He is here to take our sins upon Him and die for our sins.

This is the gospel message, the good news, Jesus came as the Lamb of God to take our sins. The next time you see someone struggling with their sin and in need of forgiveness, can you share this simple message? "Behold! The Lamb of God."

Notes:

Come And See – John 1:35-39

J ohn the Baptist cannot help talking about Jesus as the Lamb of God. When he does this with a couple of his followers nearby, they leave John and go follow Jesus.

> *35 Again, the next day, John stood with two of his disciples. 36 And looking at Jesus as He walked, he said, "Behold the Lamb of God!"*
>
> *37 The two disciples heard him speak, and they followed Jesus. 38 Then Jesus turned, and seeing them following, said to them, "What do you seek?"*
>
> *They said to Him, "Rabbi" (which is to say, when translated, Teacher), "where are You staying?"*
>
> *39 He said to them, "Come and see." (John 1:35-39a)*

Jesus asks a very poignant question, "What do you seek?" In other words, what do you want?

This really is the key question. If God would ask you today, *What do you want?* What would you say? We often think of God as a heavenly Santa Claus who will give us our heart's desire. Well yes and no. We often think that what we want is a thing. Something like more money, a better job, or a better relationship. These are all good things, but much of the time, God wants to go much deeper. The disciples sort of got this when they asked, "Where are You staying?" In other words, they wanted to spend time with Jesus. They wanted to get to know Jesus better. They wanted a relationship with Him.

Interestingly, Jesus' response to the question is "Come and see." He does not say where He is staying because He does not have a home, He is a traveling rabbi. He does not have a home address, but He does know how to navigate through life so that your life can be filled with joy. He is offering a life that is filled with peace that comes from a forgiven heart. He is offering a life that is filled with overflowing love for others.

Is this something that you want today? If so, the only way to get it is to become one of His followers. You may have to give up some stuff in your life. Can you do that? What will be the hardest thing to give up so that you can "Come and see"?

Notes:

A Wedding - John 2:1-5

Jesus and His disciples are invited to a big and important party, a town wedding. Weddings in Jesus' day last for days and days. There is a lot of food, celebrating, and of course wine. However, disaster strikes.

> *¹ On the third day there was a wedding in Cana of Galilee, and the mother of Jesus was there. ² Now both Jesus and His disciples were invited to the wedding. ³ And when they ran out of wine, the mother of Jesus said to Him, "They have no wine."*
>
> *⁴ Jesus said to her, "Woman, what does your concern have to do with Me? My hour has not yet come."*
>
> *⁵ His mother said to the servants, "Whatever He says to you, do it. (John 2:1-5)*

Jesus' mother, Mary, is also at this wedding celebration. Unfortunately, on the third of the wedding celebration, they run out of wine. Oddly enough, Mary wants Jesus to fix the problem. Jesus knows that this is not on His agenda, but for His love for his Mother, He agrees. The most interesting line in this dialog is Mary's; *"Whatever He says to you, do it."*

There is no clearer description of what it means to be one of His disciples, followers, and students – Do what He says.

The servants are told to fill the dirty, foot-washing pots with water. They are not emptied first; they are just topped off. The servants then take some of this nasty water to the master of ceremonies. We can assume that the servants are laughing under their breath at this great joke. The master of ceremonies tastes the wine and he proclaims to the groom for all to hear:

And he said to him, "Every man at the beginning sets out the good wine, and when the guests have well drunk, then the inferior. You have kept the good wine until now!" (John 2:10)

Jesus does not just change water into wine, He changes it into the good wine, the best stuff. He is still doing this today, with you and me. He takes us as we are, filled with lots of nasty dirty thoughts, broken relationships, and selfish attempts at happiness. He wants to change us into the best that we can be, from the inside out.

It is very simple and hard at the same time; *"Whatever He says to you, do it."* Can you do that today?

Notes:

Born Again? – John 3:1-3, 14-15

¹ There was a man of the Pharisees named Nicodemus, a ruler of the Jews. ² This man came to Jesus by night and said to Him, "Rabbi, we know that You are a teacher come from God; for no one can do these signs that You do unless God is with him." ³ Jesus answered and said to him, "Most assuredly, I say to you, unless one is born again, he cannot see the kingdom of God."

¹⁴ And as Moses lifted up the serpent in the wilderness, even so must the Son of Man be lifted up, ¹⁵ that whoever believes in Him should not perish but have eternal life. (John 3:1-3, 14-15)

For some, this is a story that you have heard before. But, let's look at it from a different angle. Nicodemus was a very well-educated Jewish religious leader. He knew the scriptures. He knew the Book of Ezekiel.

I will give you a new heart and put a new spirit within you; I will take the heart of stone out of your flesh and give you a heart of flesh. (Ezekiel 36:26)

Nicodemus knew that to get a new heart turned towards God, God Himself had to do the work to change the heart. This is what Jesus is getting at when He talks about being born again. That is why the end of this discussion is so important.

Then the LORD said to Moses, "Make a fiery serpent, and set it on a pole; and it shall be that everyone who is bitten, when he looks at it, shall live." (Numbers 21:8)

Jesus is referring back to Moses in the wilderness with the people of God. The people had rebelled against God, again. God sent some serpents into the desert. The people did not know what to do. God told Moses to make an image of a serpent and put it on a pole. To be healed, all the people had to do was look at it and believe.

This is another image of what it is like to be born again. When you are born, who does the work? Do you have anything to do with it?

When God changes your heart of stone into a new heart of flesh, once again, He does all of the work. The same is true with the serpent in the desert. God Himself will provide the sacrifice. All you need to do is to believe that God can do the saving work.

This is what it means to be born again, to ask for forgiveness, and then ask God to take over your life and set you on a new path. Can you explain this to someone today?

Notes:

For God So Loved – John 3:16

John 3:16 is a very familiar verse in the Bible. However, we often put the emphasis on the wrong person in the verse.

For God so loved the world that He gave His only begotten Son, that whoever believes in Him should not perish but have everlasting life. (John 3:16)

Notice how the verse starts, it starts by talking about what God did. God loved, and He gave. However, we often read it like God gave to ME! We read this verse like we are very lovable people, so of course God would love and give. However, Paul gives us a different perspective in his letter to the Church in Rome.

6 For when we were still without strength, in due time Christ died for the ungodly. 7 For scarcely for a righteous man will one die; yet perhaps for a good man someone would even dare to die. 8 But God demonstrates His own love toward us, in that while we were still sinners, Christ died for us. 9 Much more then, having now been justified by His blood, we shall be saved from wrath through Him. 10 For if when we were enemies we were reconciled to God through the death of His Son, much more, having been reconciled, we shall be saved by His life. 11 And not only that, but we also rejoice in God through our Lord Jesus Christ, through whom we have now received the reconciliation. (Romans 5:6-11)

Paul gives us a very clear description of who we really are. We are "without strength, ungodly, sinners, and enemies." These are not the kind words that we usually use to describe ourselves. We often think, *"Of course, God would send His Son to die for me. I deserve it, don't I?"* However, we see here who we really are to God. We are against Him, unloving, and in fact, His enemies. When we read John 3:16 in this context, it has a much bigger impact.

We do not deserve God's love, or Jesus' sacrifice. We do not deserve everlasting life; in fact, we deserve to perish into eternal darkness.

So, the next time you hear this verse, put the emphasis on the correct actor, God. It is not about us and what we deserve, but it is about what God did out of His boundless mercy.

Given this perspective, what do you think about the phrase, *"whoever believes in Him"?* What do you think it means to believe in Him? How would (should) this change your actions?

Notes:

Love Darkness – John 3:18-21

Jesus continues His discourse on the love of God, light, and darkness.

> ¹⁸ *"He who believes in Him is not condemned; but he who does not believe is condemned already, because he has not believed in the name of the only begotten Son of God.* ¹⁹ *And this is the condemnation, that the light has come into the world, and men loved darkness rather than light, because their deeds were evil.* ²⁰ *For everyone practicing evil hates the light and does not come to the light, lest his deeds should be exposed.* ²¹ *But he who does the truth comes to the light, that his deeds may be clearly seen, that they have been done in God."* (John 3:18-21)

Jesus reminds his disciples that He is the Light of the World that has come to extinguish the darkness. However, we love the darkness over the light. Why do we love the darkness? Because it hides our daily thoughts and actions.

We sometimes call these the "skeletons in the closet." It is said that we all have them. That is, we all have some things that we want to hide from others. For much of our lives, we think that we can hide these wicked thoughts and actions from God.

Jesus is telling his disciples while this is a common attitude, it is still very foolish. We love the darkness; we love hiding from God. We do not want our innermost thoughts to be exposed. Therefore, we hate the light and we try to hide in the darkness.

Jesus wants us to come into the light. But, how do we do this? First, we must believe that we stand condemned before God. We believe that we know what is best for our lives, and we do not want to listen to God or depend on Him. Once we acknowledge that we have been living and hiding in the darkness, we must come to the light. This means believing that God sent His Son to die for us because we were making a mess of our lives. Coming into the light means giving up control of our lives and allowing God to direct our paths.

Your word is a lamp to my feet
And a light to my path. (Psalm 119:105)

What do you think is the harder part of this, leaving the darkness or coming into the light? What do you need to do today to come more into the light? Do you know someone living in the darkness of deception? If so, can you bring light into their life?

Notes:

New Life - John 3:30-36

John the Baptist is fulfilling his task and purpose: to point to Jesus as the Lamb of God. John knows that his role must now diminish as the focus is on Jesus. But, what does this mean?

30 He must increase, but I must decrease. 31 He who comes from above is above all; he who is of the earth is earthly and speaks of the earth. He who comes from heaven is above all. 32 And what He has seen and heard, that He testifies; and no one receives His testimony. 33 He who has received His testimony has certified that God is true. 34 For He whom God has sent speaks the words of God, for God does not give the Spirit by measure. 35 The Father loves the Son, and has given all things into His hand. 36 He who believes in the Son has everlasting life; and he who does not believe the Son shall not see life, but the wrath of God abides on him." (John 3:30-36)

John acknowledges that he must now decrease because Jesus came from above. John is answering a fundamental human philosophical question; "If God is so much bigger than we are, how can we ever get to know Him?

John knows that Jesus knows God the Father as He came from above (heaven). Jesus speaks the truth about who God is and what it means to live a Godly life, but no one listens to him, for we all love the darkness. John then emphasizes that God the Father loves God the Son and the Father has given all things into the hands of the Son. It is from this perspective that Jesus leads His ministry on Earth. He will show us, over and over again, what it means to love the Lord your God with all our heart, soul, and mind.

Jesus tells everyone that the kingdom of heaven is at hand, it is here now, with Him. He gives everlasting life. That is a new life that starts now and goes on forever. This new life does not wait until we are dead, but He changes our hearts and then our lives now.

How does this happen? It happens when we "believe in the Son." This is deeper than believing just what He says. Believing in Him means that we put our faith and trust in Him, that He will change our hearts and then our lives. This trust begins a new life that lasts forever. If we do not put our trust in Him, we shall not see this new life but we will receive the wrath of the Father.

This is quite a choice; a new life with Jesus or God the Father's wrath. What do you choose? Now, go explain this choice to a friend or neighbor.

Notes:

Liar or Messiah? - John 4:5-8, 25-26

J esus has a long discussion with a woman, in the heat of the day, while she goes about a simple everyday task of drawing water. At the end of this discussion, Jesus declares Himself to be the Messiah. Let's see how this unfolds.

> *5 So He came to a city of Samaria which is called Sychar, near the plot of ground that Jacob gave to his son Joseph. 6 Now Jacob's well was there. Jesus therefore, being wearied from His journey, sat thus by the well. It was about the sixth hour.*

> *7 A woman of Samaria came to draw water. Jesus said to her, "Give Me a drink." 8 For His disciples had gone away into the city to buy food.*

> *25 The woman said to Him, "I know that Messiah is coming" (who is called Christ). "When He comes, He will tell us all things."*

> *26 Jesus said to her, "I who speak to you am He." (John 4:5-8, 25-26)*

Samaria is a despicable place for devout Jews. The Samaritans are religious half-breeds and the religious leaders in Jerusalem will not have anything to do with them. Jesus, on the other hand, sits at the well at high noon (the sixth hour) looking for a drink of water. Jesus begins the discussion by simply asking for a drink of water. They then have a religious discussion about ethnic bias, worship, and a fulfilled life. Jesus offers her living water that will satisfy her beyond just her physical needs. Jesus then confronts her about the choice of men in her life. You can read the full dialog in John 4:5-42.

The woman knows that the Messiah is coming and He will resolve all of these issues; ethnic bias, how to worship, and how to have a fulfilled life. Jesus very clearly declares to her that He is the Messiah.

If you or friends of yours have doubts about Jesus' Messiahship, this is just one of the places where Jesus' Messiahship is declared. Over and over again Jesus made declarations that He is the living water, the bread of life, the resurrection, and the life. There is no doubt that Jesus declared Himself the Messiah. Therefore, everyone has a simple choice; either Jesus is a delusional lair or the Messiah. He cannot just be a good teacher or prophet because no good teacher teaches lies about themselves nor would a prophet of God. The choice is simple – crazy man or Messiah. There is no middle ground. How would you describe this dilemma to a friend of yours?

Notes:

Your Son Lives - John 4:46-54

Jesus did a number of miracles during His time of ministry in Israel. But, why did He do the miracles that He did? What was the point?

46 So Jesus came again to Cana of Galilee where He had made the water wine. And there was a certain nobleman whose son was sick at Capernaum. 47 When he heard that Jesus had come out of Judea into Galilee, he went to Him and implored Him to come down and heal his son, for he was at the point of death. 48 Then Jesus said to him, "Unless you people see signs and wonders, you will by no means believe."

49 The nobleman said to Him, "Sir, come down before my child dies!"

50 Jesus said to him, "Go your way; your son lives." So the man believed the word that Jesus spoke to him, and he went his way. 51 And as he was now going down, his servants met him and told him, saying, "Your son lives!"

52 Then he inquired of them the hour when he got better. And they said to him, "Yesterday at the seventh hour the fever left him." 53 So the father knew that it was at the same hour in which Jesus said to him, "Your son lives." And he himself believed, and his whole household.

54 This again is the second sign Jesus did when He had come out of Judea into Galilee. (John 4:46-54)

Jesus was back in Cana, where He previously had been at the wedding party. A certain nobleman, who was a powerful and influential man, ran up to Jesus and implored that He heal his son. Jesus used an odd expression about signs and wonders.

The Greek word *semeion* is typically translated as miracles or signs. This narrative ends by describing this as the second sign that Jesus did.

The primary purpose of the miracle, or sign, is surprisingly not to heal someone; but to point; for that is what signs do, they point. The purpose of these signs is to point from Jesus, God's Son, to God the Father. They are to bring glory and honor to God so that everyone; the healed one, their family members, and the observers would give glory to God the Father and then realize that Jesus is His Son.

We often miss this in our daily lives. Think of all of the little things that God is doing in your life; from keeping you from harm, to bringing you joy, or saving you from making the wrong choice. When you think about these things, can you see them as pointing you to God the Father? How will you now acknowledge what He is doing in your life?

Notes:

What Do You Want? – John 5:1-7

Jesus encountered many people during His ministry who had lots of needs. It wasn't very often when He asked, "Do you want to be made well?"

¹ After this there was a feast of the Jews, and Jesus went up to Jerusalem. ² Now there is in Jerusalem by the Sheep Gate a pool, which is called in Hebrew, Bethesda, having five porches. ³ In these lay a great multitude of sick people, blind, lame, paralyzed, waiting for the moving of the water. ⁴ For an angel went down at a certain time into the pool and stirred up the water; then whoever stepped in first, after the stirring of the water, was made well of whatever disease he had. ⁵ Now a certain man was there who had an infirmity thirty-eight years. ⁶ When Jesus saw him lying there, and knew that he already had been in that condition a long time, He said to him, "Do you want to be made well?"

⁷ The sick man answered Him, "Sir, I have no man to put me into the pool when the water is stirred up; but while I am coming, another steps down before me." (John 5:1-7)

This seems like a very odd question to pose to the man, *"Do you want to be made well?"* At first blush, it would seem that a man who was there for thirty-eight years would want to be made well. Of course, he would want to run, and jump, and dance; wouldn't he? However, if he was made well, he could no longer sit and beg for a living. After all, he had a great spot near the pool, in the shade, with lots of foot traffic. It would be very frightening to leave this sick world, the only world that he knows, to go out into the larger world and make his way.

He might be thinking; *"What would I do for a living? How would I get trained? Will it be hard to get around in the larger world that I do not know?"*

Notice that he does not answer Jesus' question, but just tries to bring up his excuses.

So it is with us sometimes. We have our own addictions, patterns in life, and our own crowd of friends. Do we have to give these up to follow Jesus? Is this what He expects? If so, do we want to be made well? Perhaps this is what Jesus is talking about when He says;

...he who loses his life for My sake will find it. (Matthew 10:39)

If Jesus were to ask you tonight; *"Do you want to be made well?"*, what would you say?

Notes:

Blessed Day - John 5:16-18

Jesus has just healed a paralyzed man, who is now walking around the Temple praising God. The religious, "righteous" Jews are furious with Jesus. But what has He done wrong?

16 For this reason the Jews persecuted Jesus, and sought to kill Him, because He had done these things on the Sabbath. 17 But Jesus answered them, "My Father has been working until now, and I have been working."

18 Therefore the Jews sought all the more to kill Him, because He not only broke the Sabbath, but also said that God was His Father, making Himself equal with God. (John 5:16-18)

The religious Jews are furious with Jesus for two reasons. The first is that He has done good and merciful acts on the Sabbath. The Jewish leaders have a mistaken view of resting on the Sabbath. The Sabbath rest comes from Genesis:

1 Thus the heavens and the earth, and all the host of them, were finished. 2 And on the seventh day God ended His work which He had done, and He rested on the seventh day from all His work which He had done. 3 Then God blessed the seventh day and sanctified it, because in it He rested from all His work which God had created and made. (Genesis 2:1-3)

God rested on the seventh day from creating. However, He is not done. He is still active after His time of creating, He is blessing and sustaining all that He made. The Sabbath rest for us is meant as a time to focus on who God is, what He has done in our lives, and to praise Him for this. This praise can be going to a worship service. It can also mean reaching out to others in need, as Jesus did in this story.

The second reason that Jews are furious with Jesus is that he puts Himself on the same level as God the Father. The idea of Jesus being equal with God the Father is blasphemy, worthy of the death penalty.

What do we take from this? First, we are not God, nor are we on His level. However, we are His ambassadors of reconciliation. We are always to be about His work, perhaps even on the Sabbath.

Can you take some time to rethink your Sabbath time? What do you do besides worship? Do you use the time being God's ambassador, doing His work of loving others? What might you add to your Sabbath routine to love and honor Him more deeply?

Notes:

Bread of Life - John 6:5-9, 12-14, 34-35

Jesus has been teaching a large crowd of about 5,000 men all day. Everyone is hungry, so Jesus asks His disciples to feed them all.

5 Then Jesus lifted up His eyes, and seeing a great multitude coming toward Him, He said to Philip, "Where shall we buy bread, that these may eat?" 6 But this He said to test him, for He Himself knew what He would do.

7 Philip answered Him, "Two hundred denarii worth of bread is not sufficient for them, that every one of them may have a little."

8 One of His disciples, Andrew, Simon Peter's brother, said to Him, 9 "There is a lad here who has five barley loaves and two small fish, but what are they among so many?"

[Jesus feeds everyone and they eat to their fill.]

12 So when they were filled, He said to His disciples, "Gather up the fragments that remain, so that nothing is lost." 13 Therefore they gathered them up, and filled twelve baskets with the fragments of the five barley loaves which *were left over by those who had eaten. ¹⁴ Then those men, when they had seen the sign that Jesus did, said, "This is truly the Prophet who is to come into the world."*

³⁴ Then they said to Him, "Lord, give us this bread always."

³⁵ And Jesus said to them, "I am the bread of life. He who comes to Me shall never hunger, and he who believes in Me shall never thirst (John 6:5-9, 12-14,34-35)

As He often does, Jesus accentuates His teaching with a real-world example. This is the first of His "I am" messages. In this case, He is the bread of life. We all know what it means to be physically hungry, but that is not what Jesus is talking about here. He is talking about the hunger for real meaning in life. Close relationships with others that count. People to love and people who love us. Knowing what our purpose in life is. This is the bread that Jesus offers us. Like in this story, we must take of the bread and eat. We must believe and trust in Jesus for the answers.

What gnawing questions about life do you have? Are you ready to try the bread of life? If so, what is stopping you?

Notes:

Walks on Water - John 6:15-21

Jesus has had a hard day. After a day of teaching and performing miracles, the people want to make Him king to kick out the Roman soldiers. Jesus will have none of that, so he sends His disciples out early so that He can have some quiet time as He will join them later.

15 Therefore when Jesus perceived that they were about to come and take Him by force to make Him king, He departed again to the mountain by Himself alone.

16 Now when evening came, His disciples went down to the sea, 17 got into the boat, and went over the sea toward Capernaum. And it was already dark, and Jesus had not come to them. 18 Then the sea arose because a great wind was blowing. 19 So when they had rowed about three or four miles, they saw Jesus walking on the sea and drawing near the boat; and they were afraid. 20 But He said to them, "It is I; do not be afraid." 21 Then they willingly received Him into the boat, and immediately the boat was at the land where they were going. (John 6:15-21)

A third of Jesus' disciples are seasoned fishermen. They know the Sea of Galilee. They know that strong winds can come out of nowhere. They are now rowing against the wind and making poor progress.

They are beginning to think that they will never make it to the other shore. They are worn out! Then, out of nowhere, Jesus comes walking on the water, up to the boat. Their first reaction is total fear, which is somewhat surprising. After all, they have seen Jesus perform lots of miracles in His ministry. However, they are learning that it is one thing to observe a miracle, it is quite another to be in the middle of one.

Once Jesus clams them down, they haul Him into the boat. What is surprising about this narrative from John, the Gospel writer, is that he does not focus on the wind or the sea. He does not tell us if the wind clams down or not. What he does focus on is the trip, and how life works out. John tells us that immediately they were at the other shore!

The point of this narrative is focus. If we are focused on the problems, in this case, the waves and the wind, that is all we will see. Over and over again, Jesus gives us illustrations of our focus. He tells us to not focus on the problems in life but to keep our focus on Him. As Matthew tells us in his Gospel, *"Seek first the kingdom of God and His righteousness..." (Matthew 6:33).*

Sure, you have problems in life. That is expected. So don't focus on them. What would it take for you to switch your focus to seek God and His kingdom?

Notes:

The Father Draws Us – John 6:41-44

John sneaks in some deep theological ideas captured in some of Jesus' discourses. One such idea occurs right after the feeding of the five thousand.

> *41 The Jews then complained about Him [Jesus], because He said, "I am the bread which came down from heaven." 42 And they said, "Is not this Jesus, the son of Joseph, whose father and mother we know? How is it then that He says, 'I have come down from heaven'?"*

> *43 Jesus therefore answered and said to them, "Do not murmur among yourselves. 44 No one can come to Me unless the Father who sent Me draws him; and I will raise him up at the last day. (John 6:41-44)*

The Jewish religious leaders are confused and upset with Jesus. They wonder how Jesus can be both the son of Joseph, the carpenter, and at the same time the One who comes down from heaven.

Things get even more confusing when the Jewish leaders consider how someone becomes one of Jesus' followers. Is Jesus just like the other traveling rabbis where you can join up for a bit and then when you get tired of Him, you can just move on?

Jesus says that it goes much deeper than that. Jesus' followers come because God the Father draws them to Jesus. The Greek word, *helkuo,* can be translated as draw, pull vigorously, or to drag. In our individualistic, take charge, world this language seems strange to us. However, it makes more sense when we consider the original twelve apostles whom He called. He called them specifically to join Him. Also, with Paul on the road to Damascus, God specially called him to stop persecuting the Christians and to join them.

The end result for those who God has drawn to Jesus is that they will be raised up on the last day to join Him in heaven forever.

If you think God is drawing you to Jesus, can you stop resisting Him? There is a short prayer at the end of the book to help you make this last step.

If you think that God has already drawn you to Jesus, what is the next step that He is drawing you to do? What does He have for you to do before the last day? If you know, what is stopping you?

Notes:

Who To Follow? - John 6:66-69

Jesus has been giving the religious leaders, and the disciples, some hard teachings. He has said that He is the bread of life and that He will give life forever. Many of His hearers, turn and leave in disgust.

⁶⁶ From that time many of His disciples went back and walked with Him no more. ⁶⁷ Then Jesus said to the twelve, "Do you also want to go away?"

⁶⁸ But Simon Peter answered Him, "Lord, to whom shall we go? You have the words of eternal life. ⁶⁹ Also we have come to believe and know that You are the Christ, the Son of the living God." (John 6:66-69)

Jesus is a peripatetic rabbi, a traveling rabbi. As such, it takes a real commitment to stay with Him as one of His followers, His students. You have to be with Him all of the time; walking, ministering, and learning.

Jesus confronts the twelve men that He specifically called and asks them if they want to leave and abandon Him too.

Peter has a very interesting response. He does not say; *"Where shall we go?";* rather he says; *"To whom shall we go?"* Peter knows that He is following a person. He is not on a journey to end up somewhere special; however, he is on a journey to become a new person altogether. He is following

Jesus because He has the words of eternal life. He is the Messiah, the Son of God the Father.

How many people today who are leaders have the words of life, much less the words of eternal life? Many of our leaders today are influencers. They get their title from the idea that they will influence the lifestyles of others. Perhaps they will get them to buy some new products, particularly products that will make them look better. But, do they tell us how to be better people? Do they tell us new ways to love our neighbors? Do they tell us new ways to do "unto others as you would have them do unto you?"

Jesus came to change lives, not only here on earth, but forever and ever. Have you ever thought deeply about what this means, to follow Jesus, to hang on His every word?

Read all of John 6, the whole chapter, and see what Jesus means about following Him, listening to Him, and taking in the words of eternal life.

How will you change your thinking after reading that one chapter?

Notes:

Words of Authority - John 7:40-51

It is the time of the Festival of the Booth, one of the three great festival times in Jerusalem. This is a time to celebrate what God has done in the past and to look forward to what He will do in the future.

40 Therefore many from the crowd, when they heard this saying, said, "Truly this is the Prophet." 41 Others said, "This is the Christ."

But some said, "Will the Christ come out of Galilee? 42 Has not the Scripture said that the Christ comes from the seed of David and from the town of Bethlehem, where David was?" 43 So there was a division among the people because of Him. 44 Now some of them wanted to take Him, but no one laid hands on Him.

45 Then the officers came to the chief priests and Pharisees, who said to them, "Why have you not brought Him?"

46 The officers answered, "No man ever spoke like this Man!"

47 Then the Pharisees answered them, "Are you also deceived? 48 Have any of the rulers or the Pharisees believed in Him? 49 But this crowd that does not know the law is accursed."

50 Nicodemus (he who came to Jesus by night, being one of them) said to them, 51 "Does our law judge a man before it hears him and knows what he is doing?" (John 7:40-51)

Jesus teaches with words of authority and wisdom and the Jewish leaders do not want to hear anything about it. The big debate is over where Jesus came from. How odd. Yes, He taught a great deal in the north, in Galilee; but He was born in Bethlehem, near Jerusalem, the City of David.

The chief priests want to arrest Jesus, so they send the temple officers to do this. However, these officers come back amazed because no one has taught like this Man before. They understood what Nicodemus was saying, the Man deserves to be heard.

We sometimes have the same preconceptions today. We have our ideas of who Jesus is, and what it means to be a good follower. Yet, Jesus is telling us today to listen to Him, for no one speaks like He does.

Do you need to put some of your preconceived ideas aside and really listen to Jesus? If you do this, what do you think He will be telling you?

Notes:

Who Is He? – John 7:40-44

The Jewish religious leaders had been teaching about the coming of the Messiah for many, many years. The Messiah was going to come to the people of God and set them free. However, they could not agree on how the Messiah would do this, or even who the Messiah would be. Would He be easily recognized and understood or would He be more of a mystery?

Here Jesus is in the middle of a discourse with the religious leaders.

> 40 Therefore many from the crowd, when they heard this saying, said, "Truly this is the Prophet." 41 Others said, "This is the Christ."
>
> But some said, "Will the Christ come out of Galilee? 42 Has not the Scripture said that the Christ comes from the seed of David and from the town of Bethlehem, where David was?" 43 So there was a division among the people because of Him. 44 Now some of them wanted to take Him, but no one laid hands on Him. (John 7:40-44)

The title, Christ, is the Greek term for the Hebrew title Messiah. Some of the crowd think that Jesus is indeed the Messiah, the Christ.

Others are not so sure. Jesus has spent much of His ministry in Galilee, which is far to the north of

Jerusalem and Bethlehem. The religious leaders know that the Messiah must come from the town of Bethlehem, David's town. Which the religious leaders have forgotten, is where Jesus was born.

Some of the religious leaders want to take Him and kill Him because He is leading many away from their strict Jewish faith. They cannot understand how the true Messiah would do this.

There is a great message here for all of us about our expectations of God. We often have a very clear idea of who God is and how He should act. But what if our expectations are not correct? If Jesus were to come into your place of worship next week, would you recognize Him? If He came in as a wandering homeless teacher, which He was, how would you treat Him?

In one of Jesus' parables, he talks about surprise visits.

'Assuredly, I say to you, inasmuch as you did it to one of the least of these My brethren, you did it to Me.' (Matthew 25:40)

Do you have some incorrect expectations about God that you need to shed? If so, what are they?

Notes:

Throw The First Stone – John 8:2-9

Early in the morning, Jesus went into the temple to pray and worship; unfortunately, the scribes and Pharisees had a different idea.

2 Now early in the morning He came again into the temple, and all the people came to Him; and He sat down and taught them. 3 Then the scribes and Pharisees brought to Him a woman caught in adultery. And when they had set her in the midst, 4 they said to Him, "Teacher, this woman was caught in adultery, in the very act. 5 Now Moses, in the law, commanded us that such should be stoned. But what do You say?" 6 This they said, testing Him, that they might have something of which to accuse Him. But Jesus stooped down and wrote on the ground with His finger, as though He did not hear.

7 So when they continued asking Him, He raised Himself up and said to them, "He who is without sin among you, let him throw a stone at her first." 8 And again He stooped down and wrote on the ground. 9 Then those who heard it, being convicted by their conscience, went out one by one, beginning with the oldest even to the last. And Jesus was left alone, and the woman standing in the midst. (John 8:2-9)

The religious leaders brought in a woman, without the man, to Jesus as she was caught red-handed in the act of adultery. The religious leaders wanted to get Jesus caught on the horns of a dilemma. Either He would violate Roman law, which did not allow the Jews to commit capital punishment, or He would violate Jewish law and let the woman off of the hook. What to do?

Jesus proceeded to take the attention away from the woman and write in the dirt. No one knows what He wrote, but perhaps it was a list of common sins such as; anger, hatred, deceit, lying, coveting, envy, untrustworthy, or just being unloving.

One by one, they saw their own sins on the ground and realized that they too needed forgiveness. The oldest one got it first and eventually even the youngest one got it.

If you were in this crowd, what sin would you have seen on the ground that would have struck you deep in your heart? When would you have left; near the beginning and at the end? If later in the day, you saw the woman, what would you have said to her?

Notes:

Light of the World - John 8:12

The concept of light goes through the entire Bible, from the very beginning in Genesis to the view of heaven in the Book of Revelation. So, what does it mean when Jesus calls Himself the light of the world?

> Then Jesus spoke to them again, saying, "I am the light of the world. He who follows Me shall not walk in darkness, but have the light of life." (John 8:12)

Genesis starts with God creating all that is by starting with light.

> [1] In the beginning God created the heavens and the earth. [2] The earth was without form, and void; and darkness was on the face of the deep. And the Spirit of God was hovering over the face of the waters. [3] Then God said, "Let there be light"; and there was light. [4] And God saw the light, that it was good; and God divided the light from the darkness. (Genesis 1:1-4)

In the beginning, there is just God; God the Father, God the Son, and God the Holy Spirit. The first thing that they create is light. It is not the universe, the Earth, or mankind, but light. This light is different from the darkness, it divides it. John begins his Gospel with light:

⁴ In Him was life, and the life was the light of men. ⁵ And the light shines in the darkness, and the darkness did not comprehend it. (John 1:4-5)

In Jesus is life and light. His light is so powerful that the darkness cannot overcome it or comprehend it.

In the final book of the Bible, the temple in the New Jerusalem is described as having no light sources, except for the glory of God. What does that have to do with us and our regular daily lives? Matthew sums it up nicely:

¹⁴ "You are the light of the world. A city that is set on a hill cannot be hidden. ¹⁵ Nor do they light a lamp and put it under a basket, but on a lampstand, and it gives light to all who are in the house. ¹⁶ Let your light so shine before men, that they may see your good works and glorify your Father in heaven. (Matthew 5:14-16)

We are to be the light of the world, each and every day. We are never to hide the light of life that Jesus produces in our hearts, but we are to shine so that others will see our good works and give glory to God. What might you do today to let your light shine?

Notes:

Freedom - John 8:31-36

Jesus talks a great deal about truth and freedom. These are big lofty words, but what do they mean? What is He driving at when He talks about freedom?

> *31 Then Jesus said to those Jews who believed Him, "If you abide in My word, you are My disciples indeed. 32 And you shall know the truth, and the truth shall make you free."*
>
> *33 They answered Him, "We are Abraham's descendants, and have never been in bondage to anyone. How can You say, 'You will be made free'?"*
>
> *34 Jesus answered them, "Most assuredly, I say to you, whoever commits sin is a slave of sin. 35 And a slave does not abide in the house forever, but a son abides forever. 36 Therefore if the Son makes you free, you shall be free indeed. (John 8:31-36)*

This is a very famous statement from Jesus; *'You shall know the truth, and the truth shall make you free."* He expands on it by responding to the shocked response from the religious leaders. They immediately refer to their lineage, they are descendants of Abraham, the father of the Jewish nation. Oddly, they say that they have never been in bondage to anyone, as their ancestors were in bondage in Egypt for four hundred years. Perhaps, what they mean is that they, personally, have not been in bondage to anyone, they are their own free agents.

Jesus is quick to point out that there are several different types of bondage. He is pointing out that as sinners, we are a slave to our own sin. Sometimes it is being caught in a series of lies that we can no longer get out of. Sometimes it is an addiction to drugs, alcohol, gambling, gossip, or other acts of pleasure that have truly captured our hearts. Sometimes it is our own addiction to personal status or power, where it seems that everything that we do is only to improve our influential social position.

Jesus closes this description of freedom by addressing where we live. He says that the freedom that He brings allows us to live in the house of the Lord forever. This is a house where we are free to be the person that we were created to be, not the phony made-up character that we often portray.

Imagine putting your phony masks away forever. Being exposed for who you truly are, and actually liking it. This truth of who we are is one aspect of this phrase from Jesus about freedom.

Are there areas in your life or your character where you feel that you are in bondage to sin? Can you confess these to Jesus and ask for His help in breaking the bonds? What is stopping you?

Notes:

Whose Sin Caused This? - John 9:1-3

I n Jesus' day, people thought that calamities, such as physical ailments, were caused by someone's sin. In the case of this man who was born blind, everyone was wondering, what did his parents do to cause this?

¹ Now as Jesus passed by, He saw a man who was blind from birth. ² And His disciples asked Him, saying, "Rabbi, who sinned, this man or his parents, that he was born blind?"

³ Jesus answered, "Neither this man nor his parents sinned, but that the works of God should be revealed in him. (John 9:1-3)

While Jesus has previously acknowledged that sin has consequences, and we often have to reap what we sow; this case is different. Jesus declares that in this situation, God was going to do a mighty work.

In this story of the man born blind, Jesus heals him, but He did it on the Sabbath. The religious authorities are furious with Jesus for this infraction of the man-made Sabbath law. They interrogate the healed man about who Jesus is and what He did.

³⁰ The man answered and said to them, "Why, this is a marvelous thing, that you do not know where He is from; yet He has opened my eyes! ³¹ Now we know that God does not hear sinners; but if anyone is a worshiper of God and does His will, He

hears him. ³² Since the world began it has
been unheard of that anyone opened the
eyes of one who was born blind. ³³ If this Man
were not from God, He could do nothing."
³⁴ They answered and said to him, "You were
completely born in sins, and are you teaching
us?" And they cast him out. (John 9:30-34)

The man born blind declares that Jesus must be
from God, for how else could He do this miraculous
sign? The religious authorities do not want to hear
anything about Jesus and His works from the
"nobody", so they cast him out. Later, he runs into
Jesus again.

³⁵ Jesus heard that they had cast him out;
and when He had found him, He said to
him, "Do you believe in the Son of God?"
³⁶ He answered and said, "Who is He, Lord,
that I may believe in Him?" ³⁷ And Jesus said
to him, "You have both seen Him and it is He
who is talking with you." ³⁸ Then he said,
"Lord, I believe!" And he worshiped Him.
(John 9:35-38)

Jesus tells the man that he has seen the Son of
God. This is a wonderfully ironic statement to a man
born blind. So, it may be for us; God has a great work
in store for us, but we just need to acknowledge it.
Can you open your spiritual eyes and see?

Notes:

The Door – John 10:1-7

Jesus spent a great deal of time in the countryside, often with farmers and shepherds. His audience knew about the shepherds' life and how to care for sheep. That is what makes this illustration by Jesus so powerful.

> *¹ "Most assuredly, I say to you, he who does not enter the sheepfold by the door, but climbs up some other way, the same is a thief and a robber. ² But he who enters by the door is the shepherd of the sheep. ³ To him the doorkeeper opens, and the sheep hear his voice; and he calls his own sheep by name and leads them out. ⁴ And when he brings out his own sheep, he goes before them; and the sheep follow him, for they know his voice. ⁵ Yet they will by no means follow a stranger, but will flee from him, for they do not know the voice of strangers." ⁶ Jesus used this illustration, but they did not understand the things which He spoke to them. ⁷ Then Jesus said to them again, "Most assuredly, I say to you, I am the door of the sheep. (John 10:1-7)*

Jesus says that He is the door for the sheep, but what does this mean?

The sheepfold in this illustration is the place where the sheep spent the night. At night, the sheep are most vulnerable to attack. They need someplace where they are protected.

The sheepfold has walls of stone or thorny branches and just one doorway in and out. It is not unusual for the shepherd to sleep in the doorway and hence make himself the door. Once the sheep are settled in the sheepfold for the night, they know that they are safe. That is why, in the morning, they will happily follow their shepherd for they know his voice.

Jesus uses this illustration to show what kind of relationship He wants to have with His followers. He is the One who provides safety and security. He knows that we will encounter strangers, thieves, and robbers in life. They are trying to steal joy and security from us. Jesus wants us always to remember that our main defense is the door. He will keep the evil one at bay. Though we "walk through the valley of the shadow of death", He will be with us, protecting us all along the way.

When you see all kinds of life's troubles trying to steal your joy, just shut the door on them to keep them out. Can you do this?

Notes:

The Good Shepherd – John 10:11-14

Jesus continues His comparison between Himself and the shepherd of the sheep. He uses some very bold and comforting descriptions.

> ¹¹ *"I am the good shepherd. The good shepherd gives His life for the sheep.* ¹² *But a hireling, he who is not the shepherd, one who does not own the sheep, sees the wolf coming and leaves the sheep and flees; and the wolf catches the sheep and scatters them.* ¹³ *The hireling flees because he is a hireling and does not care about the sheep.* ¹⁴ *I am the good shepherd; and I know My sheep, and am known by My own.* (John 10:11-14)

Jesus correctly describes the role of the shepherd, which is to protect the sheep in the face of extreme danger. The hireling, the paid worker, will flee in the face of trouble. Jesus continues with this description:

> ²⁷ *My sheep hear My voice, and I know them, and they follow Me.* ²⁸ *And I give them eternal life, and they shall never perish; neither shall anyone snatch them out of My hand.* (John 10:27-28)

Jesus, the good shepherd, knows His sheep intimately; so much so that they will follow Him just by the sound of His voice.

This is the kind of relationship that Jesus desires with His followers. First, they recognize that He is leading them and He will lead them into green pastures and beside still waters. Second, even though enemies abound around them, He will protect His followers.

He knows His sheep. This means that we can bring our troubles and concerns to Him and He will hear us. The more time we spend following Him, the more we will get to know Him. He will get to know His voice, above the cacophony of the voices of the world and its influencers. We can trust His voice as we navigate our way through the world.

It is not just for today, but for all time. He promises life eternal with Him as our good shepherd. Not only that, but He will protect us so that no one can snatch us out of His hand.

The section of scripture is so very reassuring when we are unsure of what path to take. He says that our job is to listen to His voice and then follow Him. He will lead to the right path. Even if we get lost along the way, we can rest assured in His promise that no one, not even the evil one, can snatch us out of His hand. While we think that we are holding His hand, actually He holds onto us.

Remember this image of Jesus, the good shepherd. What can you do this week to make it easier for you to hear His voice?

Notes:

Waiting and Weeping – John 11

Waiting for God to move is sometimes very hard. While we are in the midst of pain and suffering, it is hard to see why God would wait. He has a good reason. Take Lazarus for example.

¹ Now a certain man was sick, Lazarus of Bethany, the town of Mary and her sister Martha.

⁵ Now Jesus loved Martha and her sister and Lazarus. ⁶ So, when He heard that he was sick, He stayed two more days in the place where He was. ⁷ Then after this He said to the disciples, "Let us go to Judea again." (John 11:1, 5-7)

Jesus' ministry takes Him outside of Bethany, the hometown of Lazarus, one of Jesus' good friends. Lazarus gets sick and he is on the verge of dying. When Jesus hears about this, He does nothing immediately. He delays. After a two-day delay, He goes to Bethany. When He gets there, it is too late, Lazarus has died.

¹⁷ So when Jesus came, He found that he had already been in the tomb four days. ¹⁸ Now Bethany was near Jerusalem, about two miles away. ¹⁹ And many of the Jews had joined the women around Martha and Mary, to comfort them concerning their brother.

20 Then Martha, as soon as she heard that Jesus was coming, went and met Him, but Mary was sitting in the house. 21 Now Martha said to Jesus, "Lord, if You had been here, my brother would not have died. 22 But even now I know that whatever You ask of God, God will give You." (John 11:17-22)

As soon as Jesus arrives, Martha chastises Jesus. *If only, Jesus you did what I wanted you to do...* Jesus ignores her barbs and goes to the tomb.

33 Therefore, when Jesus saw her weeping, and the Jews who came with her weeping, He groaned in the spirit and was troubled. 34 And He said, "Where have you laid him?" They said to Him, "Lord, come and see."35 Jesus wept. (John 11:33-35)

Jesus shares in their pain and suffering. Even though He knows that there is more to the story. At this point, He only shares in their pain.

Remember this when you are going through a very tough time. Jesus has been there. He will weep alongside you. You will walk with you through the valley of the shadow of death and He will take you to the other side. Can you hold onto this thought?

Notes:

Resurrection and Life – John 11

I n the midst of Mary and Martha's pain and suffering, Jesus has a very important message to share.

25 Jesus said to her, "I am the resurrection and the life. He who believes in Me, though he may die, he shall live. 26 And whoever lives and believes in Me shall never die. Do you believe this?" (John 11:25-26)

He is the resurrection and the life. He brings life that goes on forever. This is hard for any of us to wrap our heads around, so He gives us a physical sign that we will never forget.

39 Jesus said, "Take away the stone."

Martha, the sister of him who was dead, said to Him, "Lord, by this time there is a stench, for he has been dead four days."

40 Jesus said to her, "Did I not say to you that if you would believe you would see the glory of God?" 41 Then they took away the stone from the place where the dead man was lying. And Jesus lifted up His eyes and said, "Father, I thank You that You have heard Me. 42 And I know that You always hear Me, but because of the people who are standing by I said this, that they may believe that You sent Me." 43 Now when He had said these things, He cried with a loud voice, *"Lazarus, come forth!"* [44] *And he who had died came out bound hand and foot with graveclothes, and his face was wrapped with a cloth. Jesus said to them, "Loose him, and let him go." (John 11:39-44)*

Jesus commands Lazarus to rise from the dead and walk out of the tomb. He could have done this miracle days ago. He could have done it before He got to Bethany. However, He wanted everyone to understand in their hearts, minds, and souls, that He is the resurrection and the life.

He brings something that the world cannot. He brings a new life that begins here and now and then goes on forever. He asks Martha the key question, *"Do you believe this?"*

He asks all of us the same question. Do you really believe this? If you say that you do, how will this change your life? He did this miracle as a sign that God the Father sent Jesus to earth to live among us and then to die for our sins. If you were there in the crowd when Lazarus walked out, how would this have changed your life?

Notes:

Lazarus's Witness – John 12

After Lazarus was raised from the dead, he did not waste his new life. He got engaged with the world. We first find him at a dinner party thrown in Jesus' honor.

> *¹ Then, six days before the Passover, Jesus came to Bethany, where Lazarus was who had been dead, whom He had raised from the dead. ² There they made Him a supper; and Martha served, but Lazarus was one of those who sat at the table with Him. (John 12:1-2)*

Lazarus appears to be enjoying life with friends at a party. As it turns out, many people knew of this party and they wanted to join; but for many different reasons.

> *⁹ Now a great many of the Jews knew that He was there; and they came, not for Jesus' sake only, but that they might also see Lazarus, whom He had raised from the dead. ¹⁰ But the chief priests plotted to put Lazarus to death also, ¹¹ because on account of him many of the Jews went away and believed in Jesus. (John 12:9-11)*

Many of the local Jewish people wanted to join in with Lazarus' celebration of life. They probably had lots of questions, like: *"What was it like to be dead? What do you remember? Did you see a great light?"* It seems that Lazarus did a good job of describing what Jesus had done. He probably said more than once; *"It was not me. Jesus did it all."*

Unfortunately, not everyone took too kindly to Lazarus' witness to Jesus and who He is. The chief priests wanted to silence Lazarus and his witness, pointing to Jesus. Ironically, they wanted to put Lazarus to death.

Did they not see the irony in this? Lazarus is the one who Jesus raised from the dead. If they tried to silence him by killing him, couldn't Jesus just raise him again?

They did not understand that you cannot just turn off the light of the world. It will overpower the darkness, and the darkness will not be able to overcome the light.

I have come as a light into the world, that whoever believes in Me should not abide in darkness. (John 12:46)

This is how our witness should be. If you are born again, a new creation by the Holy Spirit, how can you not share that with your friends and neighbors? Are you sharing with such brightness that people want to kill you? If not, why not?

Notes:

Foot Washing Betrayal – John 13:2-5

One of the more dramatic lessons that Jesus gave to His apostles was the washing of their feet. In Jesus' time, everyone wore either sandals or they went barefooted. Therefore, their feet were always very dirty. This is why many homes had a pitcher of water at the entrance so that everyone could wash their feet before coming into the house. The wealthy had gentile servants who would wash the feet of the guests so that no one would be too embarrassed by the food washing act. Yet, in this case, Jesus does the foot washing.

> *2 And supper being ended, the devil having already put it into the heart of Judas Iscariot, Simon's son, to betray Him, 3 Jesus, knowing that the Father had given all things into His hands, and that He had come from God and was going to God, 4 rose from supper and laid aside His garments, took a towel and girded Himself. 5 After that, He poured water into a basin and began to wash the disciples' feet, and to wipe them with the towel with which He was girded. (John 13:2-5)*

There are several very dramatic images from this object lesson from Jesus. The first is that Jesus takes on the role of the servant even though He is their Master and Lord,. He is giving an example of the role we are called to today, servant leadership, where the leader is willing to help others, but serving them.

However, the most dramatic lesson comes from the fact that Jesus washed everyone's feet, even Judas. Jesus knew that Judas was going to betray Him in a few short hours, yet He still washed Judas' feet.

This is the same Judas who has lived, worked, and traveled with Jesus for three years. They knew each other intimately. Jesus knew all of Judas' odd mannerisms and perhaps his dry sense of humor. Judas has heard all of Jesus' teachings over these three years. He has to have come to have the head knowledge that Jesus is the long-awaited Messiah, sent by God the Father to redeem His people.

However, Judas had a heart problem. He did not want to give Jesus full control over his heart. Perhaps Judas had a money problem, and the temptation to be paid off by the religious leaders was just too great.

Judas is not that different from us. There are times when we betray our loyalty to Jesus. Often it is because of the draw of prestige, power, or influence. It is important to remember, that even when we play the role of the betrayer, Jesus will still wash our feet. He loves us that much.

Whenever you feel like God does not, cannot love you because of what you have done; can you remember this scene of Jesus washing Judas' feet?

Notes:

Love One Another – John 13:31-35

Right after the foot washing object lesson, Jesus continues with a very strong teaching message; love one another!

31 So, when he had gone out, Jesus said, "Now the Son of Man is glorified, and God is glorified in Him. 32 If God is glorified in Him, God will also glorify Him in Himself, and glorify Him immediately. 33 Little children, I shall be with you a little while longer. You will seek Me; and as I said to the Jews, 'Where I am going, you cannot come,' so now I say to you. 34 A new commandment I give to you, that you love one another; as I have loved you, that you also love one another. 35 By this all will know that you are My disciples, if you have love for one another." (John 13:31-35)

Jesus tells His apostles that He will be leaving them shortly. They will be on their own. Their beloved teacher will not be there anymore to guide them, shepherd them, or correct them. Therefore, He gives them a new commandment, actually an update to an old commandment.

... you shall love your neighbor as yourself: I am the LORD. (Leviticus 19:18b)

In Leviticus, the commandment was to love everyone, including our friends and neighbors. The commandment from Jesus was that the apostles, and by extension all of Jesus' followers, should love each other with a special love. This is the love between family members, between brothers and sisters. This love is to be stronger than the love for neighbors. This is the kind of love where we would do anything for fellow believers, perhaps even die for them.

Jesus gives a clear "how" description. If you want to know how to love your fellow believers, you are to love them just like Jesus loved His apostles. He walked with them every day. He listened to them. He taught them, often with actions and sometimes with words. He was always there for them.

Jesus also gives a clear "why" to the command. Because of the love between fellow believers, everyone will know that you are a follower of Jesus. This means your family members, your neighbors, your coworkers, and even your enemies will see Jesus in your love for fellow believers.

This seems like a very tall order. We are to have such a strong love for fellow believers that others will see it! How are you doing in this category? What can you start doing today to get more in line with what Jesus expects of you?

Notes:

My Father's House – John 14:1-4

After all of this troubling news about betrayal, a tough object lesson on servanthood, and a clear command about extreme love; Jesus talks about His Father's house. What is He trying to get at?

> *1 "Let not your heart be troubled; you believe in God, believe also in Me. 2 In My Father's house are many mansions; if it were not so, I would have told you. I go to prepare a place for you. 3 And if I go and prepare a place for you, I will come again and receive you to Myself; that where I am, there you may be also. 4 And where I go you know, and the way you know." (John 14:1-4)*

Jesus first puts His apostles' hearts at ease; "Let not your heart be troubled." Then He jumps immediately into a discussion about heaven. He is talking to His apostles, who have been walking with him mile after mile around the Israeli countryside. They have spent many nights sleeping in the open fields. They have gotten many meals of gracious handouts from people who wanted to hear more from Jesus. They probably had their fair share of rain-drenched nights with little food and empty stomachs.

So, it is interesting that Jesus does not describe heaven as an open and beautiful garden with perfect weather. Rather, He describes a city neighborhood with many houses, in fact, big and gracious houses; mansions. This must have sounded very strange to some of the apostles; such as Peter, James, and John who came from a fishing background. They did not live in mansions, but rather in smaller homes close to the fishing docks. So, why mansions?

Perhaps one reason for this might be that Jesus is trying to help them see that heaven will be a joyous place, perhaps a place with great and wonderful parties.

One of the things that we will do in heaven is see how God used many people in our lives to bring us to saving faith in Jesus. Also, we might get the privilege to see how God used us in the lives of others. All of this will be so that we can give God glory and honor more deeply and expansively.

Imagine that you have a mansion in heaven, who would you entertain there? Who might you be interested in visiting in their mansion? How might this help you give glory and honor to God?

Notes:

The Way – John 14:3-6

J esus is talking about heaven with His apostles. He gives them a very brief description of what it will be like. He then talks about the way to get there, and they are a bit mystified.

> *³ And if I go and prepare a place for you, I will come again and receive you to Myself; that where I am, there you may be also. ⁴ And where I go you know, and the way you know." ⁵ Thomas said to Him, "Lord, we do not know where You are going, and how can we know the way?" ⁶ Jesus said to him, "I am the way, the truth, and the life. No one comes to the Father except through Me. (John 14:3-6)*

Jesus is talking about preparing a place for them in heaven. He is telling them that they know the way to get there, but they are not so sure. Thomas is clearly thinking about a path or a roadway. He is looking for a map or GPS coordinates. Jesus reminds him that he has it all wrong, the way is not a path or road; the way is a person, Jesus Himself.

What does Jesus mean about being the way? Does He really mean that He is the only way? His language is very clear. *"No one comes to the Father except through Me."* Wow, this is very strong language! Well, what about the other ways that we hear about in our society today? Don't they count?

The most important thing to understand about this statement is that it is Jesus making this claim. The claim of "one way" does not come from a bunch of believers or religious leaders. It does not come from an organized religion or a church. It is not someone saying that Jesus is the way because "it is my way."

Jesus makes this claim. Based on this we can see that there are only a few choices in understanding this.

1. Jesus is confused or deluded
2. Jesus is wrong and a He is liar
3. Jesus must be the only way because He claims it to be true

If the first is true, He is just confused or deluded; then we must conclude that His other teachings are also probably confused. Then, He did not really mean that we are to love our neighbors as ourselves or turn the other cheek. Therefore, we would have to throw out His teaching ministry.

The same is true for the second opinion. If He is wrong here, what is He wrong about? It is not much of a religion if everyone can just pick and choose what to believe and how to live, is it?

That leaves us with #3. He must be the only way because He claims it to be true. What do you think about this? How would you explain this to your neighbor?

Notes:

Truth and Life – John 14:3-6

B esides His claim to be the only way into heaven, Jesus makes some dramatic claims about Truth and Life.

³ And if I go and prepare a place for you, I will come again and receive you to Myself; that where I am, there you may be also. ⁴ And where I go you know, and the way you know." ⁵ Thomas said to Him, "Lord, we do not know where You are going, and how can we know the way?" ⁶ Jesus said to him, "I am the way, the truth, and the life. No one comes to the Father except through Me. (John 14:3-6)

He clearly states how we get into heaven and truth, and life are strongly connected. This is surprising in today's post-Christian era where we have a very skeptical view of truth.

It is not unusual to hear something like this today; *"I believe that it is true, so it must be true."* This relative view of truth is an extremely naive view of life. Many things are true, whether I want them to be true or not.

For example, imagine an eight-year-old boy who believes that he is Superman. He wears Superman's costume and he runs around the house like a speeding bullet. If he went up to the roof of a ten-story building, would you let him jump off? Of course not, for you know that the law of gravity exists whether or not you want to acknowledge it.

The same is true with some moral laws. Murder is wrong in all situations. Stealing, that is taking something that is not yours from its rightful owner, is wrong. These moral laws are the basis of any well-functioning society.

Acknowledging these foundations of Truth leads to a full and abundant life. This is something that we are missing in our society today. For example, the rate of suicide is much higher with young people than it has ever been. Almost half of the young people in America have thought about a personal suicide plan. A plan!

Many of our youth today have lost the connection between Truth and Life. They need your help. Do you want to come alongside a young person and talk about Truth and Life? If so, the first step is to listen to them. Try to understand what they think about Truth and Life. Try to see where they may have a big hole in their thinking. Then, share some of your life stories. Perhaps a time when you were lost. Perhaps a time when you found Truth and how it helped to set you on a better life path.

Can you do this? You better do it before it is too late.

Notes:

Do Anything – John 14:12-14

Jesus taught a great deal about prayer. In this case, He gives a surprisingly powerful summary. "I will do it."

12 "Most assuredly, I say to you, he who believes in Me, the works that I do he will do also; and greater works than these he will do, because I go to My Father. 13 And whatever you ask in My name, that I will do, that the Father may be glorified in the Son. 14 If you ask anything in My name, I will do it. (John 14:12-14)

Most of the time, when we read this last verse, we put the emphasis on "anything." However, Jesus meant for the emphasis to be on "in My name." What is He getting at here?

One good way to deeply understand this phrase is to remember the prayer-square. The prayer-square helps us to remember at least four of the components of prayer.

The first is adoration or praise. This aspect of prayer is not for God but for us. Adoration of God helps us to remember who He is. He is the all-powerful One, the all-knowing One, the One in charge. As much as we might want it, we are not in charge of the universe.

The second side is thanksgiving. He wants us to be thankful for the big things that He has done for us, as well as the small things. He wants us to have grateful hearts. When we are grateful, we are more receptive to His word, and we are more loving to our neighbors.

The third side is confession. He is serious about us confessing our sins to Him daily. We need to continually place our sins before Him, ask for His forgiveness, and then move on with a clean heart.

The fourth side is supplication, or asking. For many of us, this is the biggest side of our "square", which means that it is not a very good square at all.

If we have balanced the other three sides of the prayer-square, we are ready to ask things of Jesus and we are ready to ask "in His name." Asking in His name is shorthand for asking in His will. We are asking in a way that will give Him glory and honor. We are asking with a grateful heart, thankful for all that He has done for us already. We are asking with a clean heart, where we have confessed many of our selfish attitudes to Him and asked for His forgiveness. Now we are ready to ask for "anything in His name."

When you look at your prayer time, do you see a balanced prayer-square? If not, is it obvious what aspect of your prayers is exaggerated? Don't think about making that aspect smaller, rather think about how you can make the other sides as big as the exaggerated one. How will you go about doing this?

Notes:

A Helper – John 14:15-18

Jesus follows His teaching on balanced prayer, with a very surprising announcement, He is sending another Helper.

15 "If you love Me, keep My commandments. 16 And I will pray the Father, and He will give you another Helper, that He may abide with you forever— 17 the Spirit of truth, whom the world cannot receive, because it neither sees Him nor knows Him; but you know Him, for He dwells with you and will be in you. 18 I will not leave you orphans; I will come to you. (John 14:15-18)

Jesus describes the Holy Spirit, as another Helper. Jesus, of course, is the first Helper. But He cannot be everywhere and with everyone in His physical form on earth. Therefore, the Father is sending the Holy Spirit.

We see first that the Holy Spirit is someone who will abide, that is live with God's people forever. We can always count on Him being with us.

He is the Spirit of truth. As Jesus was the way, the truth, and the life; the Spirit will be the One who helps us see the truth each and every day. We can count on Him when the world has lost its way concerning the truth.

The Holy Spirit is the One who will indwell us, that is to live inside our hearts. As Jesus has said earlier,

He is going back to the Father and He will reign at the Father's right hand. The Father and the Son, have assigned the Holy Spirit the task of indwelling each of His true believers. He will be the Helper. He will help us understand the Scripture and have them grow in our hearts. For example, David prayed;

Open my eyes, that I may see Wondrous things from Your law. (Psalm 119:18)

Later, Paul gave a wonderful short prayer;

17 that the God of our Lord Jesus Christ, the Father of glory, may give to you the spirit of wisdom and revelation in the knowledge of Him, 18 the eyes of your understanding [heart] being enlightened; that you may know what is the hope of His calling, what are the riches of the glory of His inheritance in the saints, (Ephesians 1:17-18)

The prayers here are that the Holy Spirit would indwell our hearts and minds and open them and our understanding so that we might see the riches of His glory. This is just one of the roles of the Indwelling Holy Spirit, that He might illumine our hearts and give us understanding. With this, we can rest in God's arms as His children. Are you ready to do this?

Notes:

Teach and Remember - John 14:25-28

Jesus explains that two of the specific tasks of the Holy Spirit are to teach and help remember.

25 "These things I have spoken to you while being present with you. 26 But the Helper, the Holy Spirit, whom the Father will send in My name, He will teach you all things, and bring to your remembrance all things that I said to you. 27 Peace I leave with you, My peace I give to you; not as the world gives do I give to you. Let not your heart be troubled, neither let it be afraid. 28 You have heard Me say to you, 'I am going away and coming back to you.' If you loved Me, you would rejoice because I said, 'I am going to the Father,' for My Father is greater than I. (John 14:25-28)

Jesus again calls the Holy Spirit the Helper, or the Comforter. He is going to help and bring comfort with two specific tasks.

First, He is going to teach the apostles and by extension all of His believers. It is pretty clear that the apostles do not know or understand everything that Jesus taught them. They still have a great deal to learn about turning the other cheek, praying for and loving their enemies, and forgiving seventy times seven times. Much of life is filled with difficult trials and temptations. Much of the time, we do not know what to do. But, if we ask the indwelling Holy

Spirit to use each occasion as a teaching moment, He will.

The second task of the Holy Spirit is to help us remember all of the things that Jesus has taught us. This is especially important when we are angry or overly passionate about a situation. These are the times when we are not thinking very clearly. During these times, if we ask Him, the Holy Spirit will help us remember things that we already know.

Right after this instruction on the Holy Spirit, the Helper, and Comforter, Jesus tells us that He has a new kind of peace for us. This peace is not anything that we can get from the world, that means, we cannot get this peace from our work, from being successful, from making lots of money, or from having important associates. This is one of the gifts that we get from the indwelling Holy Spirit as He teaches us and helps us to remember.

Whenever you are flustered, harried, or not sure what to say or do; take a breath and whisper a prayer to the Holy Spirit and ask Him to help you remember what you have been taught. Remember, take a short breath and offer a quick prayer for help.

Notes:

Abide in Me – John 15:1-8

Jesus uses a horticultural object lesson to describe what a living relationship with Him looks like. Imagine walking through a vineyard early in the season when the vines are being pruned and trimmed so that they will be ready for the growing season.

> *¹ "I am the true vine, and My Father is the vinedresser. ² Every branch in Me that does not bear fruit He takes away; and every branch that bears fruit He prunes, that it may bear more fruit. ³ You are already clean because of the word which I have spoken to you. ⁴ Abide in Me, and I in you. As the branch cannot bear fruit of itself, unless it abides in the vine, neither can you, unless you abide in Me.*
>
> *⁵ "I am the vine, you are the branches. He who abides in Me, and I in him, bears much fruit; for without Me you can do nothing. ⁶ If anyone does not abide in Me, he is cast out as a branch and is withered; and they gather them and throw them into the fire, and they are burned. ⁷ If you abide in Me, and My words abide in you, you will ask what you desire, and it shall be done for you. ⁸ By this My Father is glorified, that you bear much fruit; so you will be My disciples. (John 15:1-8)*

In this section, Jesus uses the word "abide" six times. He really wants to be sure that His apostles get the correct picture. The Greek word, *memo,* is rich in meaning. It means to dwell, remain, be present, or be held.

He is painting the picture of a branch being attached to the main vine. He is the vine and we are the branches. We get our nourishment, our lifeblood from the true vine. If we do not dwell or remain present with Him, then we will be like the branches that have been cut off and are lying on the ground, ready to be gathered up to be burnt up in the fire.

There are only two options here. Get connected to Jesus like your life depended on it or be cast out to be burnt up. If you want to have a fruitful life, a life filled with the fruit of the Spirit, *"love, joy, peace, longsuffering, kindness, goodness, faithfulness, gentleness, and self-control (Galatians 5:22)* then you need to abide with Jesus.

How do you do this? First, tell Him that you need His help to abide with Him. Then, start each day by asking Him how you can be more present in His world like you are living and dwelling with Him. Look for ways in which He is making His fruit grow in our life and look for lessons that He is teaching you through trials and tribulations.

Notes:

Love and Joy Perfected – John 15:9-11

Jesus continues His object lesson concerning branches abiding with the vine. Now He clearly connects love, abiding, and following His commandments, with a life filled with joy.

> ⁹ *"As the Father loved Me, I also have loved you; abide in My love.* ¹⁰ *If you keep My commandments, you will abide in My love, just as I have kept My Father's commandments and abide in His love.*

> ¹¹ *"These things I have spoken to you, that My joy may remain in you, and that your joy may be full. (John 15:9-11)*

We do not normally think of the words; love, abiding, doing commandments, and joy being tied together. But Jesus is endeavoring to make sure that His apostles get the connection.

Jesus reminds us that we are loved. We are loved by the Father through the Son. We can think of this love with the picture of Jesus holding onto our hands. In this case, abiding means to keep our hands in His. We are not to try to pull away, or to run away; we are to rest in His love for us.

How do you know that you are resting in His love? Simple, you have a heart to do His things. You actually want to love your neighbor as you love yourself. You want to do unto others as you would have them do unto you. You even want to be patient during troubling times. You will even see His love growing in your heart over time. When you look back on your life, you will see times when you exhibited goodness or gentleness where you know you would not have done so in the past. You are learning to abide in His love.

When we do this, He promises that His joy will remain in, or abide in us. And not just a little bit, but our joy will be full!

Joy is not the same thing as happiness. Happiness is typically determined by outward circumstances, like when we are recognized or win a prize. Joy on the other hand is something that comes from inside of us. It is not dependent on or determined by outward circumstances. In fact, we will see over time that this inward joy grows inside us, filling us up so that we can be joyful when outward circumstances are not going our way.

We are to do His works because His love is growing in our hearts. When we do this, He will fill us up with His joy.

What can you do today to turn your life around so that you are doing His work because of His love for you, and not to try to yearn His love? For you cannot earn more of His love, you already have it all. Abide in His love and see your joy increase.

Notes:

Your Advantage – John 16:5-11

J esus has many surprising declarations, and perhaps the most surprising is that it is to our advantage that Jesus left the earth. How can this be?

> 5 *"But now I go away to Him who sent Me, and none of you asks Me, 'Where are You going?' 6 But because I have said these things to you, sorrow has filled your heart. 7 Nevertheless I tell you the truth. It is to your advantage that I go away; for if I do not go away, the Helper will not come to you; but if I depart, I will send Him to you. 8 And when He has come, He will convict the world of sin, and of righteousness, and of judgment: 9 of sin, because they do not believe in Me; 10 of righteousness, because I go to My Father and you see Me no more; 11 of judgment, because the ruler of this world is judged. (John 16:5-11)*

Jesus has made it clear to His apostles that He is leaving and returning to His rightful place in heaven with the Father. Jesus knows that the apostles are devastated by this news. Nevertheless, His comforting words are that it is very good that He is leaving. How can He say this? He spent three years with the apostles; walking, teaching, and performing miracles. It was a great time. None of the apostles can imagine how it would be better without Jesus. Yet, Jesus is emphatic that it is to their advantage because, with His departure, the Holy Spirit will come to them.

The Holy Spirit has many tasks. He will help them remember Jesus' words and His encouragement. He will help them to pray. He will help keep them on the right path. However, in this section, Jesus reveals another of the Spirit's tasks. He will convict the world of its sin. Why is this important?

When Jesus leaves, He leaves his apostles and then us in charge. We are the ones who are going to show the world God's love by how we love each other. Our chief job is not to convict the world of its sin. We are not to be the chief judge of the world, that is God's job.

So often we think we need to tell people of their sin. While that may be appropriate some of the time, what is more important is for us to be vessels of God's love. Jesus made it clear what our chief task is:

> *34 A new commandment I give to you, that you love one another; as I have loved you, that you also love one another. 35 By this all will know that you are My disciples, if you have love for one another." (John 13:34-35)*

How are you doing in letting the Holy Spirit convict others of their sin, while you focus on loving your brothers and sisters in Christ?

Notes:

Waiting – John 16:16-22

Most of the time we do not do well at waiting. We want God to act on our timeline, like now, or immediately! The apostles had to struggle with this.

16 "A little while, and you will not see Me; and again a little while, and you will see Me, because I go to the Father."

17 Then some of His disciples said among themselves, "What is this that He says to us, 'A little while, and you will not see Me; and again a little while, and you will see Me'; and, 'because I go to the Father'?" 18 They said therefore, "What is this that He says, 'A little while'? We do not know what He is saying."

19 Now Jesus knew that they desired to ask Him, and He said to them, "Are you inquiring among yourselves about what I said, 'A little while, and you will not see Me; and again a little while, and you will see Me'? 20 Most assuredly, I say to you that you will weep and lament, but the world will rejoice; and you will be sorrowful, but your sorrow will be turned into joy. 21 A woman, when she is in labor, has sorrow because her hour has come; but as soon as she has given birth to the child, she no longer remembers the anguish, for joy that a human being has been born into the world. 22 Therefore you now have sorrow; but I will see you again and your heart will rejoice, and your joy no one will take from you. (John 16:16-22)

Jesus describes His crucifixion and resurrection as a childbirth. The apostles wanted to know what a little while would be like, just as when a child is to be born, we want to when he or she will come. We keep asking "Is it time?"

Then the birth comes and it is a very painful event. Like Jesus' crucifixion, when the apostles wept bitterly and the world rejoiced. But, three days later Jesus rose from the dead and appeared to the disciples, appearing to the women first. Perhaps that was His way of acknowledging their pain in childbirth and the great joy that comes with giving birth.

Jesus makes it clear that after His resurrection, the disciples will rejoice and rejoice greatly as they will be filled with joy. Perhaps He wants us to think of His resurrection and our born-again experience like the new birth of a baby. The baby does not get everything right on day one, nor does the baby know everything. The baby needs to grow in his or her relationship with the parents. Likewise, we need to grow in our relationship with God.

Take some time to think about your born-again experience and your growth. Focus on the joy that Jesus brings. Now that you are growing, can you wait a little while for God to work His plan with you?

Notes:

Glorify – John 17:1-5

In this chapter in John's Gospel, he lets us listen in on Jesus praying. Jesus begins this prayer by talking about glory.

¹ Jesus spoke these words, lifted up His eyes to heaven, and said: "Father, the hour has come. Glorify Your Son, that Your Son also may glorify You, ² as You have given Him authority over all flesh, that He should give eternal life to as many as You have given Him. ³ And this is eternal life, that they may know You, the only true God, and Jesus Christ whom You have sent. ⁴ I have glorified You on the earth. I have finished the work which You have given Me to do. ⁵ And now, O Father, glorify Me together with Yourself, with the glory which I had with You before the world was. (John 17:1-5)

You will notice that in this introduction to His prayer, He uses "glorify" four times, in different ways. The word glory or glorify is not used much today, partly because it is such a rich word. Glory or glorify can be used to capture ideas like praise, honor, magnify, great pleasure, power, dazzling brightness, magnificence, or great beauty.

So, what Jesus is referring to in the opening sentence is how the Father honors and magnifies the Son, as the Son brings honor and majesty to the Father. Remember, the Father and Son have been in a perfect, loving relationship from all time; before the universe was created. Jesus relinquished some of His glory when He came down to earth to be born as a human baby, but now He is going back to the heavenly court.

Part of the glory that Jesus will regain is the great pleasure He gets when the people of God are saved and granted eternal life with Him and the Father. That is why He is going through the pain, torture, and separation on the cross, so that we may know the Father in a perfect relationship for all of eternity.

Jesus is looking forward to the time, just a few days ahead, when He will have finished His work of redemption. This is how He wants us to pray, by giving Him glory, honor, praise, and rejoicing in His pleasure, power, and dazzling brightness. Jude gives a great way to glory in our prayers.

24 Now to Him who is able to keep you from stumbling, And to present you faultless Before the presence of His glory with exceeding joy,
25 To God our Savior, Who alone is wise, Be glory and majesty, Dominion and power, Both now and forever.
Amen. (Jude 24-25)

Pray like this!

Notes:

In The World – John 17: 9,15-16

Jesus makes a clear distinction between His followers and the world. He makes it clear that there is a spiritual battle going on between the prince of the world and Himself. In this battle, He has a task for His followers.

> *9 "I pray for them. I do not pray for the world but for those whom You have given Me, for they are Yours.*

> *15 I do not pray that You should take them out of the world, but that You should keep them from the evil one. 16 They are not of the world, just as I am not of the world. (John 17:9,15-16)*

Jesus makes it clear to His apostles that He is praying for them. In fact, He is praying for His followers in a very special way. The first message from this section is this – know that Jesus is placing your name and your needs before the heavenly throne. He is praying for you by name.

The second message is that He is praying for us because we are in the world, the place of the spiritual battlefield. His prayer is that we will be protected from the evil one, the prince of the air.

So, you might wonder, why not just take us out of the world once we become believers? Why not be born again straight into heaven?

This is because Jesus has a task for us while we are here in the world. One of the ways that Paul describes this is with the word ambassador.

*Now then, we are ambassadors for Christ,
as though God were pleading through us:
we implore you on Christ's behalf, be
reconciled to God. (2 Corinthians 5:20)*

Jesus wants us to be ambassadors. Ambassadors are sent to a foreign land to represent the king. That is exactly what is going on here. Peter describes the battleground with the image of a roaring lion.

*Be sober, be vigilant; because your
adversary the devil walks about like a
roaring lion, seeking whom he may devour
(1 Peter 5:8*

This is the world that Jesus wants us to be in and He wants us to be His ambassadors. This is why He is praying for us.

The message is clear. We will have tough times being in the world, but it is where we are supposed to be. We just need to remember that Jesus is praying for us each and every day.

If you could listen in on Jesus' prayers, what would you like to hear? Can you tell Him this right now?

Notes:

Because of Our Love – John 17:20-23

Jesus continues to share His prayers with the apostles and surprisingly, He mentions you and me.

20 "I do not pray for these alone, but also for those who will believe in Me through their word; 21 that they all may be one, as You, Father, are in Me, and I in You; that they also may be one in Us, that the world may believe that You sent Me. 22 And the glory which You gave Me I have given them, that they may be one just as We are one: 23 I in them, and You in Me; that they may be made perfect in one, and that the world may know that You have sent Me, and have loved them as You have loved Me. (John 17:20-23)

Jesus specifically mentions you and me, those who come to believe because of the early work of the apostles. Jesus does not pray for just the apostles who are present with Him, but He prays for all those who will come to faith in the future.

Jesus has a very specific prayer for us. His prayer is that we might be one. From the vision of this oneness, the world will come to believe that Jesus was sent by the Father to redeem us from our sins.

Jesus is not talking about getting rid of all of the denominations in the church today, although I am sure there are some that He would like to see go by the wayside. He is talking about His believers acting like real brothers and sisters. Paul talks about this in his letter to the Church in Rome.

15 For you did not receive the spirit of bondage again to fear, but you received the Spirit of adoption by whom we cry out, "Abba, Father." 16 The Spirit Himself bears witness with our spirit that we are children of God, 17 and if children, then heirs—heirs of God and joint heirs with Christ, if indeed we suffer with Him, that we may also be glorified together. (Romans 8:15-17)

Jesus wants us to act like we are adopted into the family of God. We are His children, and we are to call Him "Daddy." Once we really come to believe that we are adopted, by Him, into His family; we can begin to deeply love our brothers and sisters. When our friends and neighbors see this deep love we have for other Christians, no matter what their church, economic background, or skin color; they will want to know more about the family of God and our part in it.

This is the special prayer that Jesus has for us. Now that you know this, what is one thing you can do today to show your love for a fellow believer?

Notes:

I Am He – John 18:1-6

There are several great "I am" statements that Jesus uses about Himself. I am the good shepherd, I am the light of the world, and I am the bread of life; for example. In the Garden of Gethsemane, He uses the most surprising one.

¹ When Jesus had spoken these words, He went out with His disciples over the Brook Kidron, where there was a garden, which He and His disciples entered. ² And Judas, who betrayed Him, also knew the place; for Jesus often met there with His disciples. ³ Then Judas, having received a detachment of troops, and officers from the chief priests and Pharisees, came there with lanterns, torches, and weapons. ⁴ Jesus therefore, knowing all things that would come upon Him, went forward and said to them, "Whom are you seeking?"

⁵ They answered Him, "Jesus of Nazareth."

Jesus said to them, "I am He." And Judas, who betrayed Him, also stood with them. ⁶ Now when He said to them, "I am He," they drew back and fell to the ground. (John 18:1-6)

Judas brought the religious leaders and some Roman soldiers to the Garden of Gethsemane to arrest Jesus. Jesus identifies Himself to the crowd of men who came to arrest Him. They knew why they were there. They generally knew who Jesus was. They knew what they were supposed to do, but they could not.

In that one phrase, "I am He," Jesus captures all of who He was. He is more than the good shepherd, the light of the world, and the bread of life; He is the Messiah; the One sent by the Father to set His people free, to pay the ransom for their sins. When they heard Jesus' declaration, they all fell to the ground. They were overcome by their own sinful humanness, and they knew that they could not stand before the Holy Lamb of God.

They quickly "recovered" and remembered who they were, why they were there, and that they had a job to do; they were there to arrest Jesus.

So it is with us sometimes. We get a glimpse of who God is in all of His power, splendor, and holiness. We drop down in a moment of pure worship. But then, life crashes in around us. We know that we need to get back to what needs to be done, as we have so many things to take care of.

Take a minute to imagine that you were in the garden with Judas and the crowd. Imagine that you take in the full presence of Jesus for just a moment. Now that you got that, what are you going to do differently?

Notes:

Deniers – John 18:25-27

Jesus is led to the courtyard of the high priest. Jesus is under trial. He has done nothing wrong, but the religious leaders want to be rid of this rabble-rouser. The apostles scatter in all directions, but John and Peter follow Jesus to the courtyard. Jesus has already warned Peter that he will deny Him three times, but of course, Peter does not believe this. Jesus said that Peter would deny Him before the roster crowed in the morning. Sure enough, it comes to pass as Jesus predicted.

[25] Now Simon Peter stood and warmed himself. Therefore they said to him, "You are not also one of His disciples, are you?"

He denied it and said, "I am not!"

[26] One of the servants of the high priest, a relative of him whose ear Peter cut off, said, "Did I not see you in the garden with Him?" [27] Peter then denied again; and immediately a rooster crowed. (John 18:25-27)

Luke captures a very interesting detail about this event in his Gospel.

Immediately, while he was still speaking, the rooster crowed. [61] And the Lord turned and looked at Peter. Then Peter remembered the word of the Lord, how He had said to him, "Before the rooster crows, you will deny Me three times." ⁶² So Peter went out and wept bitterly. (Luke 22:60-62)

When the roster crowed, Jesus turned to look Peter in the eyes.

Peter is captured in the moment of denial. Not just once, or twice, but three times in quick succession. When Peter sees the look on Jesus' face, he is crushed. It is a look of recognition, the pain of rejection, and full forgiveness. Peter immediately weeps in the pain of the realization of his betrayal and for a while, he struggles with self-forgiveness.

Sometimes, we are just like Peter. We are puffed up with our own pride. We are sure that we will never do anything to hurt Jesus or deny Him. And yet, it happens. We are ashamed to stand up for Jesus in a hostile, crowded event. We downplay our involvement in our Church so that we will not come off too much as a goody-two-shoes. We minimize our reading or prayer time so that we can spend "five more minutes" on social media.

Like Peter, we need to fess up to these moments of denial. We need to fully confess them to Jesus. We need to look Jesus in the face, eye-to-eye. We need to ask for forgiveness. Do you need to take a moment to look Jesus in the face and tell Him something?

Notes:

A King – John 18:36-38

Jesus has a short discussion with Pilate, the Roman magistrate. Pilate wants to know more about Jesus. Who is He? Why is He here? And, Why are the Jewish religious leaders so upset? The discussion takes a geopolitical turn. Pilate asks. *"Are you the king of the Jews?"*

> *36 Jesus answered, "My kingdom is not of this world. If My kingdom were of this world, My servants would fight, so that I should not be delivered to the Jews; but now My kingdom is not from here."*

> *37 Pilate therefore said to Him, "Are You a king then?" Jesus answered, "You say rightly that I am a king. For this cause I was born, and for this cause I have come into the world, that I should bear witness to the truth. Everyone who is of the truth hears My voice."*

> *38 Pilate said to Him, "What is truth?" And when he had said this, he went out again to the Jews, and said to them, "I find no fault in Him at all. (John 18:36-38)*

Jesus acknowledges to Pilate that He is not only a king, but He is kingdom is outside and above Pilate's puny little kingdom.

As a king, Jesus is here to bear witness to the truth. He is to bear witness to the fact that He is the way, the truth, and the life. He is the resurrection and the life. He is the Lamb of God who takes away the sins of the world. Later on, He will return to rule over the entire earth, including Pilate's puny, little kingdom. John refers to Jesus' role as king in His Book of Revelation.

"These will make war with the Lamb, and the Lamb will overcome them, for He is Lord of lords and King of kings; and those who are with Him are called, chosen, and faithful." (John 17:14)

Jesus is not just a king; He is the Lord of lords and the King of kings. One day He will return to claim His chosen faithful ones.

He sometimes forgot this aspect of Jesus. He is indeed our King of kings and Lord of lords. We are to be faithful to this King and not the puny kings and lords of the world.

Perhaps now is a good time to sit back and reflect on the fact that Jesus is not just the King of kings, but He is your King. What is your King asking you to do today?

Notes:

Caesar's Friend – John 19:12, 15-16

Jesus is brought before Pilate. Pilate questions Him and he does not see any reason to have Jesus prosecuted and killed. But then, the Jewish people accuse Pilate of not being a friend of Caesar.

12 *From then on Pilate sought to release Him, but the Jews cried out, saying, "If you let this Man go, you are not Caesar's friend. Whoever makes himself a king speaks against Caesar."*

15 *But they cried out, "Away with Him, away with Him! Crucify Him!" Pilate said to them, "Shall I crucify your King?" The chief priests answered, "We have no king but Caesar!"*

16 *Then he delivered Him to them to be crucified. Then they took Jesus and led Him away. (John 19:12, 15-16)*

Here we have Pilate, the Roman Governor, who has all of the political power of Rome behind him, afraid of the Jews. He admits that he is trying to release Jesus, but the Jews cry out; *"If you let this Man go, you are not Caesar's friend."*

The phrase probably turned Pilate's blood cold. Caesar was a ruthless ruler. He killed family members because he feared that someone would take over his throne. He killed many enemies and some friends because he worried about maintaining his political position. Just the rumor of Pilate not holding the line for Caesar could put Pilate in a difficult position. Therefore, Pilate caved in to the political pressure from the Jews and he delivered Jesus to be crucified.

This happens today in our own political worlds. Weak leaders cave into the pressure from a special interest group because they are afraid to do the right thing. Sometimes horrible things happen when political leaders do not hold to the truth.

What can you do? You can pray for your political leaders. In Paul's first letter to Timothy, he extols us to do this.

¹ Therefore I exhort first of all that supplications, prayers, intercessions, and giving of thanks be made for all men, ² for kings and all who are in authority, (1 Timothy 2:1-2)

So, pray like someone's life depends on it.

Notes:

It Is Finished – John 19:28-30

Jesus died a torturous death. First, he was flogged with a leather whip with bits of bone and metal embedded in the ends of the whip. Then He was crucified like a common criminal of the Roman execution system. In the end, He cries out *"It is finished."*

> *28 After this, Jesus, knowing that all things were now accomplished, that the Scripture might be fulfilled, said, "I thirst!" 29 Now a vessel full of sour wine was sitting there; and they filled a sponge with sour wine, put it on hyssop, and put it to His mouth. 30 So when Jesus had received the sour wine, He said, "It is finished!" And bowing His head, He gave up His spirit. (John 19:28-30)*

What exactly was finished? First, His life on earth is finished, as He really did die on that Roman cross. Second, His ministry here on earth was over. He would no longer be walking the dusty roads of Israel with his friends. His earthly time of joking with Peter, teaching Thomas, and laughing with John would be over.

Most importantly, the task that His heavenly Father had given Him was finished. Jesus came to the earth to live a perfect life so that we could see what it means to live as someone created in the image of God. He came to show us how to love our neighbors, how to turn the other cheek, and how to look out for the poor and downtrodden.

Now, He was going to finish this task by taking on the sins of the world. That means He was going to pay the price for the sin and rebellion of all our God's people. He paid the price for Abraham's sins committed long ago, for Peter's sin of denial just a few hours ago, and for all of your sins that you committed earlier in your life and the ones that you have yet to commit.

This is why Jesus can say that He is The Way, for He paid the penalty for our sins. With His payment, we can one day stand before the Heavenly Father as our clean and perfect selves.

There is nothing else that you can do to add to the act of redemption that Jesus did. That part is finished. Now, Jesus wants us to go forth and live a life with our hearts filled with gratitude.

Can you take a moment to grasp on a deeper level what Jesus did for you and what you will now do to show your gratitude?

Notes:

Go and Tell – John 20:1-2, 11-17

Jesus was killed on a Friday. The next day, Saturday, was the worst day in the lives of Jesus' followers. Then on Sunday morning, the women went back to their regular duties, in this case finalizing Jesus' body for burial.

¹ Now the first day of the week Mary Magdalene went to the tomb early, while it was still dark, and saw that the stone had been taken away from the tomb. ² Then she ran and came to Simon Peter, and to the other disciple, whom Jesus loved, and said to them, "They have taken away the Lord out of the tomb, and we do not know where they have laid Him." (John 20:1-2)

When Mary got to the tomb with her burial spices, she saw that the stone blocking the tomb had been moved and the tomb was empty. Not knowing what to do, she ran back to Peter and John to get their help with the problem – where is Jesus' body so that she can finish her burial task? Mary returned to the tomb with Peter and John. They did their thing, and Mary stayed behind to contemplate the day's events.

" ¹¹ But Mary stood outside by the tomb weeping, and as she wept she stooped down and looked into the tomb. ¹² And she saw two angels in white sitting, one at the head and the other at the feet, where the body of Jesus had lain. ¹³ Then they said to her, "Woman, why are you weeping?" She

said to them, "Because they have taken away my Lord, and I do not know where they have laid Him." ¹⁴ Now when she had said this, she turned around and saw Jesus standing there, and did not know that it was Jesus. ¹⁵ Jesus said to her, "Woman, why are you weeping? Whom are you seeking?" She, supposing Him to be the gardener, said to Him, "Sir, if You have carried Him away, tell me where You have laid Him, and I will take Him away."

¹⁶ Jesus said to her, "Mary!"

¹⁷ Jesus said to her, "Do not cling to Me, for I have not yet ascended to My Father; but go to My brethren and say to them, 'I am ascending to My Father and your Father, and to My God and your God.'" (John 20:11-17)

At this point, Mary is given one task – Go and Tell. This is a pretty good summary of what it means to live the Christian life, "Go and tell others about His resurrection and what He has done in your life." Can you do that with someone this week?

Notes:

Seeing Is Believing – John 20:24-29

Thomas often gets a lot of grief, as he is sometimes called Doubting Thomas. Perhaps that is not the best name for Thomas. Perhaps a better descriptor for Thomas would be; careful, truth-seeker, or scientist. He wants to know things for sure.

24 Now Thomas, called the Twin, one of the twelve, was not with them when Jesus came. 25 The other disciples therefore said to him, "We have seen the Lord."

So he said to them, "Unless I see in His hands the print of the nails, and put my finger into the print of the nails, and put my hand into His side, I will not believe."

26 And after eight days His disciples were again inside, and Thomas with them. Jesus came, the doors being shut, and stood in the midst, and said, "Peace to you!" 27 Then He said to Thomas, "Reach your finger here, and look at My hands; and reach your hand here, and put it into My side. Do not be unbelieving, but believing."

28 And Thomas answered and said to Him, "My Lord and my God!"

29 Jesus said to him, "Thomas, because you have seen Me, you have believed. Blessed are those who have not seen and yet have believed." (John 20:24-29)

Thomas was not there when Jesus first appeared to His disciples, so it is not surprising that Thomas is skeptical about someone rising from the dead, and coming back to life.

He is not going to believe that Jesus has come back from the grave unless he can touch His wounds. When Jesus appears to Thomas, at first, he cannot believe his eyes, and then moments later, he falls in worship of the resurrected Jesus.

Jesus ends with a rather surprising comment for all of us. Jesus acknowledges that it is good that Thomas sees and believes. But, it is more blessed that many others, some of whom Thomas will witness to, will believe in the resurrected Jesus without actually seeing Him in the flesh. This is you and I. We believe in the resurrected Jesus and place our trust in Him because the Holy Spirit has moved in our hearts and turned our lives around. Jesus leaves us with the same message that He gave the disciples, "Peace to you."

What are you going to do with the peace that Jesus gives you?

Notes:

153 – John 21:1-3, 7-11

T he resurrected Jesus appears to the disciples, but they are still very overwhelmed, confused, and delighted all at the same time. Peter is not sure what to do, so he goes back to his old job, fishing.

¹ After these things Jesus showed Himself again to the disciples at the Sea of Tiberias, and in this way He showed Himself: ² Simon Peter, Thomas called the Twin, Nathanael of Cana in Galilee, the sons of Zebedee, and two others of His disciples were together. ³ Simon Peter said to them, "I am going fishing. (John 21:1-3)

Jesus appears on the shore and the disciple can hardly believe their eyes and ears.

⁷ Therefore that disciple whom Jesus loved said to Peter, "It is the Lord!" Now when Simon Peter heard that it was the Lord, he put on his outer garment (for he had removed it), and plunged into the sea. ⁸ But the other disciples came in the little boat (for they were not far from land, but about two hundred cubits), dragging the net with fish. ⁹ Then, as soon as they had come to land, they saw a fire of coals there, and fish laid on it, and bread. ¹⁰ Jesus said to them, "Bring some of the fish which you have just caught."

11 Simon Peter went up and dragged the net to land, full of large fish, one hundred and fifty-three; and although there were so many, the net was not broken. (John 21:7-11)

Sometimes these narratives on the resurrected Jesus seem so fantastic that they are hard to believe.

John adds this little, seemingly insignificant detail, the number of fish caught. It was a really large catch, and being fishermen; of course, they counted the number of fish in the catch so they would know what they were taking to market. John did not need to add that detail for us, but he did. Perhaps he did this to make sure that we got the importance and the down-to-earth reality of Jesus' resurrection. He really did rise from the dead and appear to his disciples.

Jesus concludes this narrative with; *"Come and eat breakfast."* He wants to be very clear that it is time to get on with life, but a new life, a born-again, resurrected life.

Whenever you are feeling lost, not sure what to believe, or what to do; can you remember one hundred and fifty-three? John wants you to hang on to the fact that this really happened.

Notes:

Feed My Sheep – John 21:15-17

The resurrected Jesus appeared to His disciples many times before He ascended into heaven. During one such time, Jesus confronts Peter about his denials.

15 So when they had eaten breakfast, Jesus said to Simon Peter, "Simon, son of Jonah, do you love Me more than these?" He said to Him, "Yes, Lord; You know that I love You." He said to him, "Feed My lambs."

16 He said to him again a second time, "Simon, son of Jonah, do you love Me?" He said to Him, "Yes, Lord; You know that I love You." He said to him, "Tend My sheep."

17 He said to him the third time, "Simon, son of Jonah, do you love Me?" Peter was grieved because He said to him the third time, "Do you love Me?"

And he said to Him, "Lord, You know all things; You know that I love You." Jesus said to him, "Feed My sheep. (John 21:15-17)

We know that Peter denied even knowing Jesus three times before Jesus was crucified. Peter must have felt horrible about this and wondered continually how he could make it right with Jesus.

Maybe this is why Jesus confronts Peter three times with the question, *"Do you love me?"* This is probably the same question that Jesus asks us much of the time.

Imagine being in your bed at night, thinking through the events of the day; and then remembering several times when you denied knowing Jesus; you ignored the nudging from the Holy Spirit to comfort the person having a hard day or you were quick and antagonistic to the person who was just trying to be nice to you.

You wonder if Jesus can really forgive you for your callous disobedience, and then you remember Peter. Jesus confronted Peter and his sins, forgave him, and then He gave Peter a mission – go feed and tend my sheep.

The same is true for you today. You sin, and therefore you must ask for forgiveness. Then you must listen, for Jesus has a mission for you. Your mission may be easy or it may be very hard, but you can rest assured that Jesus will go with you in your mission.

Is it time for you to ask for forgiveness, and then listen to the Holy Spirit for the details of your mission? When you get the details, go do it!

Notes:

Life In His Name – John 20:30-31, 21:25

J ohn ends his gospel narrative with a simple, yet powerful message.

30 And truly Jesus did many other signs in the presence of His disciples, which are not written in this book; 31 but these are written that you may believe that Jesus is the Christ, the Son of God, and that believing you may have life in His name. (John 20:30-31)

John wants us to remember that there is much more that Jesus did that he did not write down. But, what he did write down was for one purpose, that we might believe that Jesus came to earth, was born as a baby of the virgin Mary, lived a perfect life showing us how to live as we were created to be, and then dying on the cross to pay for the penalty of our sins.

John reminds us that he could not write down all that Jesus did or all that He meant to those around Him.

25 And there are also many other things that Jesus did, which if they were written one by one, I suppose that even the world itself could not contain the books that would be written. Amen. (John 21:25)

John knows that there is no way that all of the books of the world could contain the thoughts, actions, and influence that Jesus had. This is where we come in.

Jesus has written His message on our hearts and minds. He now expects us to go and live out a new and renewed life that will show others around us what it means to be born again, into a new life and a new relationship with God. Jesus wants to live a life with a heart filled with gratitude towards God and love towards our neighbors.

He wants us to go be the Light of the World, and with the light of our lives, others around us will be able to read the words of Jesus written in our hearts. These words are written so that you and your neighbors may believe that Jesus is the Christ, the Son of God, who comes to bring an abundant life.

Go and be that light.

Notes:

Concluding Thoughts

It would have been great to walk with Jesus during His time here on Earth. It would have been great to be there with Nicodemus or to see Lazarus raised from the dead. But we have something better, His Word written and given to us by John, one of His apostles. We also have the Holy Spirit indwelling our hearts; teaching us, and helping us to remember all that Jesus taught. Let is to be a great source of joy for you.

Can you go tell someone of the joy in your heart today?

Prayer to Accept Jesus

If you found this devotional book helpful and you felt God tugging at your heart, you can respond to the Holy Spirit right now.

If you have never accepted Jesus as your own personal Lord and Savior, you can do that with a simple prayer.

You can pray something like this:

"Lord Jesus, I need You. Thank You for dying on the cross for my sins. I open my heart and receive You as my Savior and Lord. Thank You for forgiving my sins and giving me eternal life. Please become the shepherd of my life. Make me to be the kind of person You want me to be. Amen."

If you have any questions, you can reach out to me at:

tstaylor.devotionals@gmail.com

May God bless you on your own spiritual journey.

The Prayer-Square

I t is sometimes difficult to keep a balanced prayer time. We know that we are to spend time in the different aspects of prayer; Adoration, Confession, Thanksgiving, and Supplication (ACTS).

Adoration. We are to acknowledge who God is and to give Him honor and glory for His sovereignty, mighty power, and lovingkindness; to name a few of His attributes.

We are to spend time Confessing our sins and asking for His forgiveness.

We are to spend time Thanking Him for all of His mercies. We are to be continually thankful for all the good things that He brings into our lives; our family, our health, and our relationship with Him. We are also to be thankful for the difficult trials and tribulations that come into our lives. We are to thank Him for His presence with us as we walk through the valley of the shadow of death. We are to be thankful for all things, at all times.

He also tells us to ask, to be engaged in supplication. We are to ask for His loving mercy for our friends, family, and neighbors. We are to ask for ourselves. We are to always ask in the spirit of giving glory and honor to Him and not to ourselves.

One way to keep a balanced prayer life is to envision a prayer-square. The prayer-square is a visual guide to help keep our prayer life balanced.

```
              Adoration
        ┌──────────────────────┐
        │                      │
S       │                      │       C
u       │                      │       o
p       │                      │       n
p       │     Abide in         │       f
l       │     Prayer           │       e
i       │                      │       s
c       │                      │       s
a       │                      │       i
t       │                      │       o
i       │                      │       n
o       │                      │
n       └──────────────────────┘
              Thanksgiving
```

Give it a try.

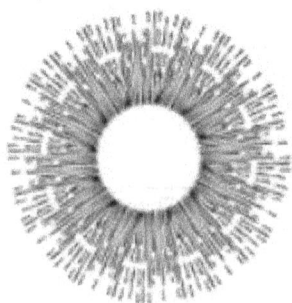

Acknowledgments

I wish to thank my class at the Church of the Apostles in Atlanta, Georgia. They worked through much of this material, as we learned from the Scriptures together.

Soli Deo Gloria

www.ingramcontent.com/pod-product-compliance
Lightning Source LLC
Chambersburg PA
CBHW071601040426

* 9 7 8 1 6 6 6 4 1 0 3 1 0 *